**This book is to be returned on or before
the last date stamped below.**

STORE

WALLINGTON LIBRARY
SHOTFIELD, WALLINGTON, SURREY
SM6 0HY   01 - 647 4458/9

RENEWALS   *Please quote:* date of return, your ticket number
and computer label number for each item.

The Citroen Dyane 6, with 602 cc air-cooled engine

Citroen 2CV, Dyane, Ami 1964-79 Autobook

By Kenneth Ball

Associate Member, Guild of Motoring Writers
and the Autobooks Team of Technical Writers

Citroen 2CV, 4, 6 1964-79
Citroen Dyane 4 1970-74
Citroen Dyane 6 1968-79
Citroen Ami 6 1964-69
Citroen Ami 8 1969-78

Autobooks Ltd. Golden Lane Brighton BN1 2QJ England

The AUTOBOOK series of Workshop Manuals is the largest in the world and covers the majority of British and Continental motor cars, as well as the majority of Japanese and Australian models.

Whilst every care has been taken to ensure correctness of information it is obviously not possible to guarantee complete freedom from errors or omissions or to accept liability arising from such errors or omissions.

CONTENTS

ISBN 0 85147 950 2

First Edition   1974
Reprinted   1974
Second Edition, fully revised   1975
Reprinted   1975
Third Edition, fully revised   1976
Fourth Edition, fully revised   1977
Reprinted   1978
Fifth Edition, fully revised   1979

789

Printed in Brighton England for Autobooks Ltd by G. Beard and Son Ltd
Bound in Hove England for Autobooks Ltd by Jilks Ltd

F

ACKNOWLEDGEMENT

My thanks are due to Citroen for their unstinted co-operation and also for supplying data and illustrations.

Considerable assistance has also been given by owners, who have discussed their cars in detail, and I would like to express my gratitude for this invaluable advice and help.

Kenneth Ball
Associate Member, Guild of Motoring Writers
Ditchling Sussex England.

INTRODUCTION

This do-it-yourself Workshop Manual has been specially written for the owner who wishes to maintain his vehicle in first class condition and to carry out the bulk of his own servicing and repairs. Considerable savings on garage charges can be made, and one can drive in safety and confidence knowing the work has been done properly.

Comprehensive step-by-step instructions and illustrations are given on most dismantling, overhauling and assembling operations. Certain assemblies require the use of expensive special tools, the purchase of which would be unjustified. In these cases information is included but the reader is recommended to hand the unit to the agent for attention.

Throughout the Manual hints and tips are included which will be found invaluable, and there is an easy to follow fault diagnosis at the end of each chapter.

Whilst every care has been taken to ensure correctness of information it is obviously not possible to guarantee complete freedom from errors or omissions or to accept liability arising from such errors or omissions.

Instructions may refer to the righthand or lefthand sides of the vehicle or the components. These are the same as the righthand or lefthand of an observer standing behind the vehicle and looking forward.

CHAPTER 1

THE ENGINE

1:1 Types, features, models, capacities

The flat twin air cooled engines with horizontally opposed cylinders and overhead valves in the Citroen Ami and Dyane vehicles are closely similar in basic design to the engines incorporated in the 2CV models (type AZ) since their inception in 1948. These developed 18 bhp (SAE) at 5000 rev/min, with bore and stroke of 66 x 62 mm, 425 cc capacity and compression ratio of 7.5:1. The CV description here indicates the taxation rating under the French fiscal system.

Referring to **FIGS 1:1, 1:2, 1:3** and **1:4,** power is transmitted direct to the front wheels from the front-mounted engine through constant velocity joints at the ends of two transmission halfshafts. The casing in which the crankshaft and camshaft revolve is of aluminium alloy and in two parts, with a vertical joint located by dowels and studs. It is connected at the bottom to the gearbox and to the clutch housing. The gearbox provides four forward synchromesh ratios and one reverse gear. The clutch is of the single dry plate type or optionally a semi-automatic centrifugal type may be provided.

The crankshaft is a steel forging consisting of five parts with two main bearings and two crankpins. It is assembled during manufacture complete with the two connecting rods and their bearing shells and built up together with the crankpins by shrink fitting after cooling the assembly down to nearly —200°C. Expansion of the parts to their normal temperature results in a permanent assembly for all practical purposes in which only the small-end bushings can be renewed. The connecting rods are steel forgings drilled over the entire length so that the undersides of the pistons are cooled by oil jets. The big-end bearings are integral with the connecting rods and hence are not supplied for servicing. Also, as the crankshaft cannot be reground undersize main bearings are not available. Renewal of any of the components involves the renewal of the whole crankshaft assembly.

The camshaft (see **FIG 1:4**) is of cast iron and runs in the crankcase below the crankshaft in two bearings. It is gear driven from the crankshaft and the thrust is carried on the front bearing. The rear bearing incorporates the body of the gear-type oil pump.

The separate opposed cylinders are of cast iron and of finned construction, each with a shoulder on which they locate in the crankcase. Provision is made at the crankshaft ends to clear the connecting rods and they are fitted

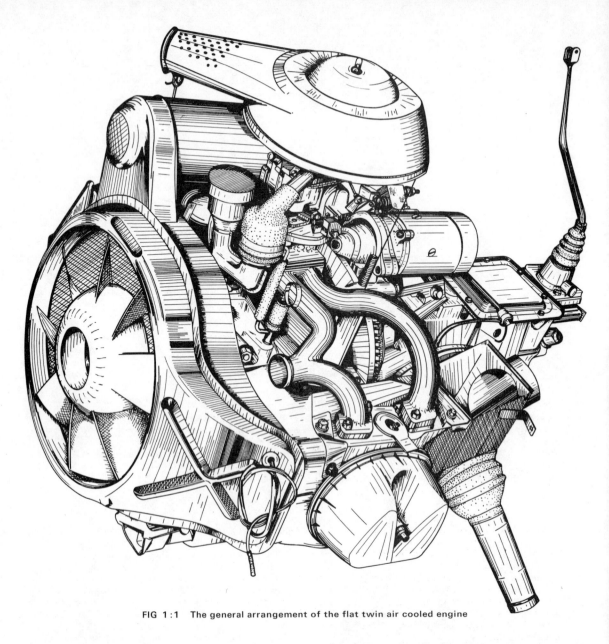

FIG 1:1 The general arrangement of the flat twin air cooled engine

without shims or gaskets. If renewal is required they are supplied in sets of two fitted complete with pistons. The cylinders cannot be rebored and new pistons are not available separately. Three piston rings, a compression ring, a scraper ring and an oil control ring are fitted. The cylinder heads are of aluminium alloy and house the valves and rocker components. No cylinder head gasket is used. The cylinder heads incorporate cast iron valve guides and valve seat inserts which are not individually renewable.

Lubrication is by a gear-type oil pump by which oil is circulated as shown in FIG 1:5 through an aluminium oil cooler at the front of the engine. The oil is carried

round the exhaust valve guides from which it flows into the cylinder heads. A relief valve regulates the pressure. Oil filtration is by means of a gauze filter in the sump and an external oil filter in later models.

The engine is cooled by the circulation of air from a metal or nylon fan contained in a housing and with a grille at the rear as shown in FIG 1:1. The air then passes through ducts to the cylinder heads and cylinders. Cooling is also assisted by the external oil cooler, over which the air propelled by the fan passes. As previously mentioned, the undersides of the pistons are cooled by jets of oil coming from drilled passages in the connecting rods and the valve guides and exhaust valves are cooled

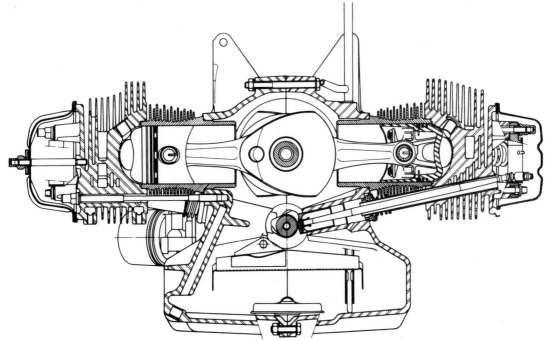

FIG 1:2 A typical vertical sectional view of the engine

by the rocker arm lubricating oil. To maintain a suitable running temperature a cover is provided for fixing over the front grille below the bonnet if the outside temperature falls below 10°C, the removal of which is advised at temperatures over 15°C.

The different vehicle and engine combinations are identified in the following text by the manufacturer's code which can be found in the chart at the end of this manual.

With the basic engine type continuing unchanged a great deal of similarity occurs in overhaul operations for all models. In this and the following chapters instructions are given for typical procedures with particular features relating to individual models being mentioned as appropriate.

1:2 Working on engine in car

Apart from normal running adjustments to the fuel and ignition systems and the generator belt tension, other work which can be undertaken without the removal of the engine includes such work as removing and dismantling the cylinder heads and cylinder assemblies, decarbonizing and overhaul of valves and rocker gear, renewing small-end bushes and attention to the generator, distributor and carburetter as necessary. Instructions on these matters are given in this and later chapters. It should be noted, however, that if both cylinder heads have to be removed it is easier to take out the engine.

Under normal driving conditions the engine lubricating oil should be changed every 5000 km (3000 miles) or 3000 km (2000 miles) if the vehicle has arduous use.

The drain plug is under the sump and is unscrewed with a 21 mm ring spanner. The sump capacity is 2.2 litre for an oil change or 2.5 litre on reassembly after dismantling. The recommended oil is of SAE 20W.40 grade or 10W.30 for very cold climates. Periodically check the oil level with the vehicle on a flat surface and at least five minutes after the engine has been switched off. The oil level should be flush with the upper shoulder on the dipstick and should never fall below the lower shoulder. There is a difference of .6 litre between the maximum and minimum marks.

For working underneath the car it is often necessary to jack it up at front or rear. In all these operations special care needs to be observed to see that the car is firmly supported by suitable blocks or stands to make sure that it will not be shaken off the jacking arrangements by such jolting as is inseparable from the work being undertaken.

1:3 Removing the engine and gearbox assembly

The engine can be removed either with or without the gearbox attached. For the former operations, proceed as follows:

1 Remove the bonnet or secure it open to its fullest extent but not touching the windscreen wipers.

2 Disconnect the battery negative cable and remove the spare wheel. Disconnect and remove the accelerator return spring.

3 Remove the inlet silencer in **FIG 1:6**. Disconnect the spring 3, the hose 1 and the retaining nuts from the bracket 6 (see **FIG 1:7**) to remove the assembly. A similar procedure applies to the later type of silencer shown in **FIG 1:8**.

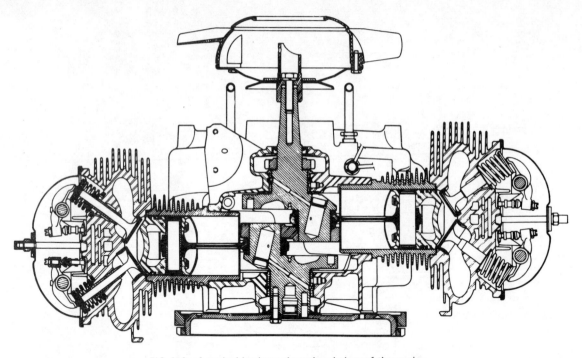

FIG 1:3   A typical horizontal sectional view of the engine

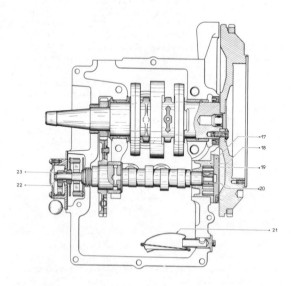

FIG 1:4   A typical longitudinal sectional view of the engine

Key to Fig 1:4   17 Oil pump cover   18 Oil pump
19 Pump gear   20 Pump gear   21 Oil filter   22 Circlip
23 Thrust·washer

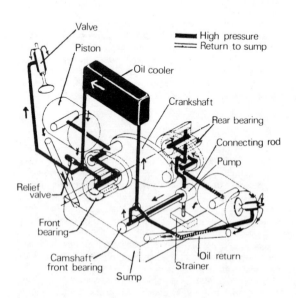

FIG 1:5   Lubrication system

4 Disconnect the wiring from the headlamps, direction indicators, the horn, the distributor, the coil and the sparking plugs. Remove the earth connections from the headlamp assembly and the gearlever support. Free the wiring harness from its clips and rest it on the lefthand wheel cover. Disconnect the leads from the starter switch terminal and from the generator.

5 Remove the heater connections after removing the securing clamps 10 and 11 in **FIG 1:9**.

6 Turn the headlight control knob anti-clockwise as far as it will go. Free the control lever valves by tilting the beam units upwards.

7 Disconnect the bonnet lock cable from the return lever on the lefthand wing cover. On the Ami 6 disconnect the tensioners.

8 Remove the retaining nuts and disconnect the front wing bodywork and the bumpers.

9 Disconnect the heating control rod 1, the spring 2 and the flexible conduit (see **FIG 1:10**).

10 Remove the carburetter choke control. Remove the cable support and disconnect the throttle control and return spring.

11 Remove the clamps securing the heat exchanger on the exhaust assembly and disconnect the silencer.

12 Disconnect the starter motor, the distributor and the regulator.

13 Disengage the accelerator pedal from its floor support.

14 Disconnect the gearchange control and the adjusting nuts of the brake cables. Disconnect the brake hose from its attachment on the gearbox. Free the clutch cable at the pedal clevis.

15 Remove the handbrake cable adjusting nuts. Remove the clamp screw and disconnect the speedometer cable.

16 Disconnect the fuel pump inlet pipe and plug the pipe opening.

17 Remove the front seat and the carpet for access to the rubber plugs sealing the rear attaching nuts of the gearbox. Turn back the tab washers and loosen these bolts by several turns.

18 Remove the clips retaining the boots to the sliding transmission shafts.

19 Remove the bolts, nuts and serrated washers, retaining the engine to the front mountings and attach suitable lifting tackle.

20 Lift the assembly sufficiently to free the rear mountings and allow the casing to clear the front crossmember. Then pull the assembly forward to release the brake cables from their locations in the front crossmember. Continue to lift the assembly until disengagement of the transmission shafts is complete and the assembly can be lifted out of the vehicle as shown in **FIG 1:11**.

To remove the engine without the gearbox, procedure is the same up to operation 20 and taking the strain on the lifting tackle, with the retaining bolts removed from the front mountings. The four nuts which secure the gearbox to the engine are then removed, with a spanner 1791.T available for unscrewing the lower nuts. Lift the engine forwards very carefully to disengage it from the gearbox, ensuring that no weight is allowed to bear on the gearbox primary shaft and that the crankcase is not damaged by the centring studs. Note that if lifting tackle is not available the engine can be lifted out by two persons, taking such precautions as described.

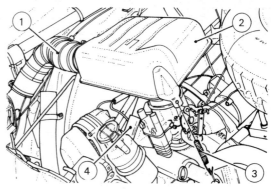

FIG 1:6 Air silencer since September, 1966

Key to Fig 1:6   1 Connecting hose   2 Silencer   3 Spring
4 Connection to breather and carburetter

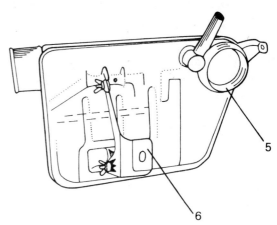

FIG 1:7 Air silencer showing support 6 and sleeve connector 5

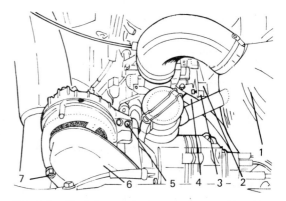

FIG 1:8 Air silencer and other details since May, 1968

Key to Fig 1:8   1 Silencer   2 Throttle control   3 Starter control   4 Fuel inlet   5 Generator adjusting bolt   6 Casing 7 Retaining bolt

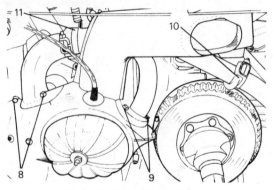

FIG 1:9   Manifold attachments

Key to Fig 1:9   8/9 Securing nuts   10/11 Clamps

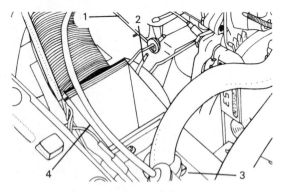

FIG 1:10 Heater assembly

Key to Fig 1:10   1 Control rod   2 Spring   3 Cover
4 Heater assembly

1:4 Removing and servicing the heads, attention to valves

To remove a cylinder head (see **FIG 1:12**) operations are undertaken as follows:

1 Disconnect the battery negative lead, unscrew the retaining nut and remove the rocker cover, with a tray or other receptacle suitably positioned to catch the oil which will be released from the cover.

2 On saloon models, remove the spare wheel and the wheel arch. On van models remove the wing and wing panel.

3 Remove the inlet silencer (see operation 3 in the previous Section).

4 Disconnect the fuel pipe and the throttle control rod from the carburetter. On vans, disconnect the rubber connection from the breather.

5 Referring to **FIG 1:13**, remove the half-casing 7 of the AC generator or alternator where fitted. Unscrew the retaining nut 7 (see **FIG 1:14**) and loosen the adjusting nut 6 to disengage the driving belt. The alternator may be left in place.

6 Referring to **FIG 1:9**, remove the clamps 10 and the

manifold securing fasteners 8 and 9. Slacken the clamp 11, which need not be removed.

7 Lift the manifold tubes out of the way with a block of wood on the crankcase. Remove the flange gaskets and plug the holes. Remove the sparking plug.

8 Remove the retaining nuts shown in **FIG 1:15** and **1:16** and the retaining nuts of the mountings to remove the upper and lower air casings. Disconnect the cylinder head lubricating pipe (see **FIG 1:17**). Note the metering screws on the cylinder head and the crankcase, the former having two holes each 7 mm diameter and the latter one hole 2 mm diameter.

9 Bring the piston into the TDC position at the end of the compression stroke, with the rockers not touching their respective valves. Remove the three retaining nuts 1 shown in **FIG 1:34**, commencing with the lower one and disengage the cylinder head.

The tappets may be removed with the aid of a hooked rod applied through one of the lubrication holes. The rocker assemblies and valves are removed as follows:

1 Referring to **FIG 1:18**, detach the rocker shaft screws 6, the distance pieces 2, the rockers 3 and the washers 4 and 5. Some types will have a slightly different rocker fitted with a spring at the lower end of the spindle. Withdraw the double rubber joint 1 (see **FIG 1:19**), the cup washers 2, the springs 3 and

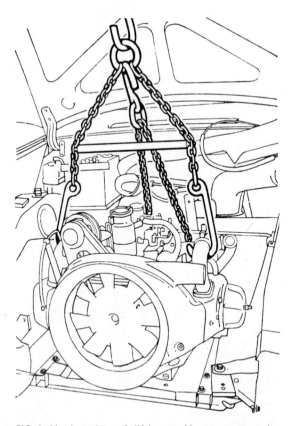

FIG 1:11   Location of lifting tackle to remove the engine

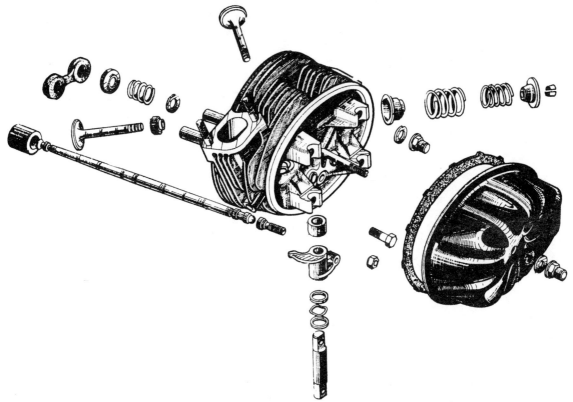

FIG 1:12   An exploded view of a cylinder head, rocker cover, rocker gear and valves

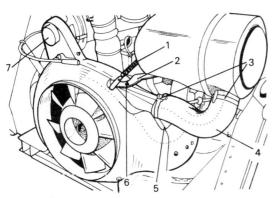

FIG 1:13   Air casing assembly

Key to Fig 1:13   1 Accelerator return spring   2 Lever
3 Clip   4 Air duct   5 Attaching nuts   6 Nut   7 Half casing

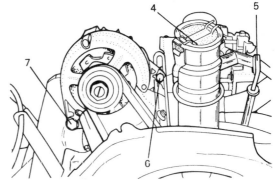

FIG 1:14   Alternator attachment

Key to Fig 1:14   4 Breather assembly   5 Dipstick
6 Alternator adjusting nut   7 Securing bolt

the washers 4 of the pushrod tubes. Keep all components in order for refitting in the same positions.
2 The springs must be compressed to enable the collets
to be removed. Owing to the angle of the valve in the
head, an ordinary compressor may prove difficult to
use in which case it may help to refit the rocker
spindle to enable the spring to be levered downwards
with a suitable implement. If the latter method is used,

the valve head must be supported in the combustion
chamber. A bolt and nut must be used to secure the
rocker spindle at the free end before applying any
force.
3 Remove the collets 7 (see **FIG 1:20**), the springs 3
and 4, the spring seats 6, the locating cups 2 and the
seals 5. Remove the assembly from the vice and
withdraw the valves and rocker shafts.

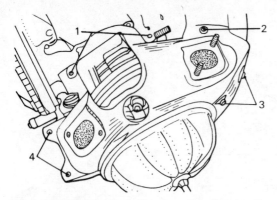

FIG 1:15 Details of cylinder air casing, showing the retaining fasteners at 1, 2, 3 and 4

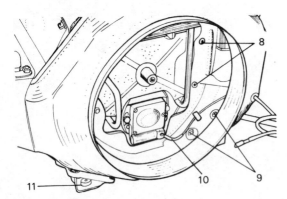

FIG 1:16 Air inlet casing with fan removed

Key to Fig 1:16   8/9 Nuts and screws   10 Distributor lead
11 Flexible supports

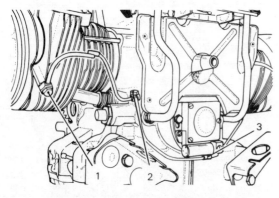

FIG 1:17   Cylinder head lubrication pipe

Key to Fig 1:17   1 Metering bolt on cylinder head
2 Metering bolt on crankcase   3 Protecting clip

4 The valve seats may be ground in using a sucker-type valve grinding tool. The specified valve seat angles are 120 deg. for inlet and 90 deg. for exhaust valves (see **FIG 1:21**). The cylinder head valve seats and valve guides are shrunk in during manufacture and if unserviceable the cylinder head complete must be renewed. It is necessary that the largest diameter of the valve seat must be equal to the greatest diameter of the valve and that the width 'I' in **FIG 1:21** should be a maximum of 1.45 mm inlet and 1.80 exhaust.

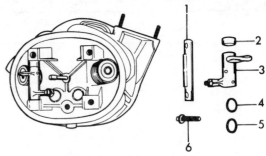

FIG 1:18   Rocker assemblies

Key to Fig 1:18   1 Spindle   2 Distance piece   3 Rocker
4 Flexible washer   5 Thrust washer   6 Rocker shaft retaining screw

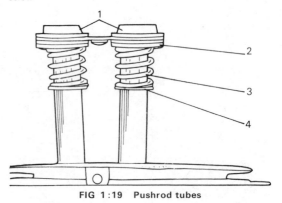

FIG 1:19   Pushrod tubes

Key to Fig 1:19   1 Double rubber joints   2 Cup washers
3 Springs   4 Seating washers

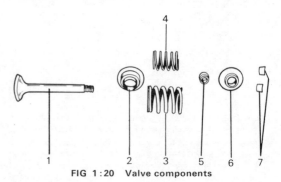

FIG 1:20   Valve components

Key to Fig 1:20   1 Valve   2 Cup   3/4 Springs   5 Seal
6 Spring seat   7 Collets

A radius of .5 mm is made on the valve head
angles at 'a' and 'b'. On completion of grinding,
ensure that the cylinder head is thoroughly clean
and that all particles of grinding material have
been removed. Also check that the oil hole in the
exhaust valve cap is clear.

Reassembly and refitting of the cylinder head is undertaken by reversing the instructions for removal and dismantling, with attention given to the following details:

1 Clean the top of the piston and the mating face of the
cylinder. No gasket is used.

2 Guide the pushrod tubes so that the shoulders on the
sealing rings enter the bores in the crankcase. Tighten
the nuts to a torque of 1.2 kg m. Oil and fit the push-
rods, checking that the ball ends are free from scores
or burrs.

3 Bring the piston to its TDC position to locate the
cylinder head in place. Run up the nuts evenly against
their flat washers until the cylinder head is in contact
with the cylinder and the cylinder in contact with the
crankcase.

4 Oil the valve stems and the seats before refitting.

5 Connect the oil pipe to the cylinder head and ensure
that the two .7 mm diameter holes in the union screw
are clear.

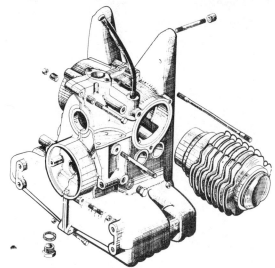

FIG 1:22 An exploded view of the cylinder and crankcase

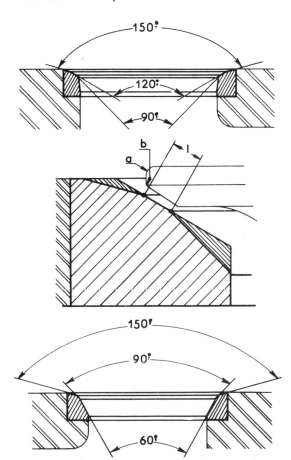

FIG 1:21 Valve seat angles

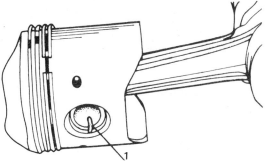

FIG 1:23 Piston and connecting rod assembly showing
a gudgeon pin circlip at 1

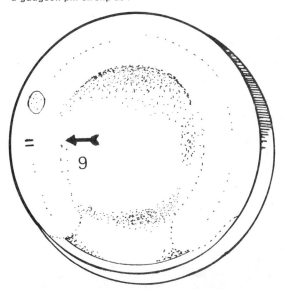

FIG 1:24 The arrow 9 on the top of the piston must
point towards the front of the engine

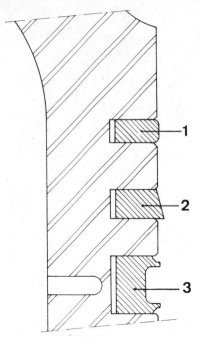

FIG 1:25 Piston rings as fitted to earlier engines

Key to Fig 1:25   1 Compression ring   2 Scraper ring
3 Oil control ring

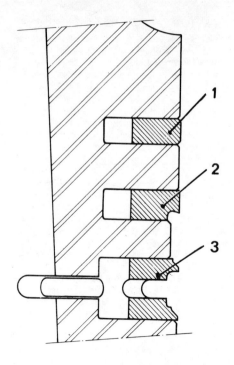

FIG 1:27 Section through piston showing the U-flex
oil control ring

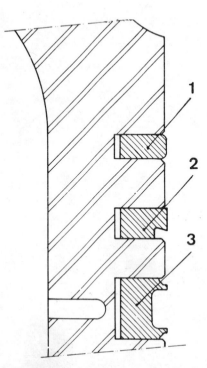

FIG 1:26 Section through piston showing later type
scraper ring

6 When positioning the manifolds and engaging the
heat exchanger on the upper cylinder head casing
smear the gasket faces with sealing compound. The
exhaust gaskets have a larger diameter than the inlet
gaskets. Tighten the nuts and bolts with shakeproof
washers to a torque of 1.4 to 1.5 kg m.

7 The final tightening torque for the cylinder head nuts
is 2 to 2.3 kg m (14.5 to 17 lb ft). On cars up to
1968 the lower nut should be tightened first and then
the two upper nuts, on later cars the two upper nuts
are tightened first. Refit in reverse procedures the
components removed and disconnected for access.

8 Adjust the rocker arm clearances with the engine cold
by means of the adjusting screws and locknuts to
give the clearance shown in **Technical Data**.

To ensure correct adjustment the operating clearance
of a valve must be measured when the corresponding
valve in the opposite cylinder is fully open.

9 To fit the rocker cover first ensure that the mating
faces are clean and dry and use a new rubber gasket,
which should be bonded to the cover with an adhesive
such as Bostic 1400. Extreme care is necessary when
fitting the cover to avoid the loss of oil contained in
the tappet chamber and circulating in the lubrication
system. Note that on some engines the rocker covers
are marked 0, which should be upwards. Tighten the
securing nut(s) to a torque of .5 to .7 kg m.

10 Top up the oil level, start the engine and check for
leaks. If necessary, adjust the idling speed (see
Chapter 2) when the engine is hot.

1:5 Removing and refitting cylinders and pistons

Each piston is selectively assembled with its cylinder. Replacement pistons are not available and only the complete assembly is renewable.

Referring to **FIG 1:22**, removal of the cylinder is undertaken by first removing the cylinder head as described in the previous Section, when the cylinder can be withdrawn from the engine assembly as shown in the illustration. The piston will remain attached to the connecting rod, which is not separable from the crankshaft (see **FIG 1:23**).

The pistons are marked with the letters D and G signifying that they are fitted on the righthand or lefthand side of the engine and with an arrow on the top (see **FIG 1:24**) which must point towards the front of the engine. The specified clearance in the cylinder bore is .05 to .07 mm. As no provision is made for reboring the cylinder replacement pistons are not available.

The earlier piston ring arrangement is shown in **FIG 1:25**, but since December 1969 a new scraper ring has been used as shown in **FIG 1:26**. It is recommended during overhaul to fit this new ring. Since June 1972 some 602 cc engines have been fitted with the U-flex oil control ring (see **FIG 1:27**), which has a larger inside diameter than the outside of the piston.

Use a piston ring remover to withdraw the rings, and check that the new rings turn freely in the grooves. Rings are marked 'Haut', 'H' or 'Top' on the upper surface near the gap and must be fitted accordingly. The rings should be fitted temporarily in the cylinders to check the gaps which should be as follows:

2CV (1) .30 to .45 (2) .25 to .40 (3) .20 to .35 mm
3CV (1) .20 to .35 (2) .10 to .25 (3) .15 to .30 mm

On reassembly the ring gaps must be arranged at 120 deg. to each other with the scraper ring gap upwards on the righthand piston and downwards on the lefthand piston. Lubricate the parts with clean engine oil and fit the cylinder over the piston using a suitable ring compressor as shown in **FIG 1:28**. The cylinder must not be turned as it is fitted as this would reposition the ring gaps. Remove the ring compressor and refit the cylinder head as described in **Section 1:4**.

Engines manufactured since October 1966 are fitted with a fully floating gudgeon pin which is located by a circlip at each end. With earlier engines the gudgeon pin is a loose fit in the connecting rod and an interference fit in the piston.

Removal of the gudgeon pin used in the earlier engines is undertaken with the use of an extractor tool such as that shown in **FIG 1:29**. Note that gudgeon pins are selectively assembled to their respective pistons and care must be taken to maintain the same combinations. Take care when removing a piston not to damage the piston skirt against the connecting rod or the cylinder head studs. The studs can be covered with hose pipe to help prevent such damage.

To refit the earlier gudgeon pin, heat the piston to about 60°C in a bath of hot oil or in an oven to allow the gudgeon pin to be inserted by hand. Locate the circlip 1 (see **FIG 1:23**) on the flywheel side of the piston after assembly, oil the gudgeon pin and insert it into the front boss so that it is located 2 to 3 mm proud of the inside face of the boss. Fit the connecting rod and complete the insertion of the pin, finally fitting the remaining circlip.

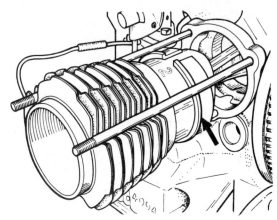

FIG 1:28 Reassembling a cylinder. The ring compressor is arrowed

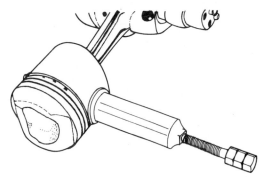

FIG 1:29 The special tool used for removing a gudgeon pin

Renewal of a small-end bush is a precise operation which it is advised should be undertaken by a service agent.

1:6 Removing clutch and flywheel

With the engine removed from the car after disconnecting the gearbox as described in **Section 1:3**, turn the engine on its side and rest it on the lefthand sidemember. Remove the clutch mechanism securing bolts and withdraw the clutch assembly. Loosen the clutch to flywheel bolts evenly one at a time until the spring pressure is released and mark the components for reassembly. The flywheel may then be removed from the crankshaft by unscrewing the retaining bolts (see **FIG 1:4**).

Examine the friction face of the flywheel for scores or cracks. Refacing should be undertaken by a suitably equipped service agent when the area on which the clutch mechanism locates must also be refaced by the same amount as the pressure plate area without removing the flywheel from the lathe, in order to ensure that the two faces are perfectly parallel. The condition of the ring gear, which is shrunk on the flywheel, should also be examined. If renewal is necessary it is advisable to use the special

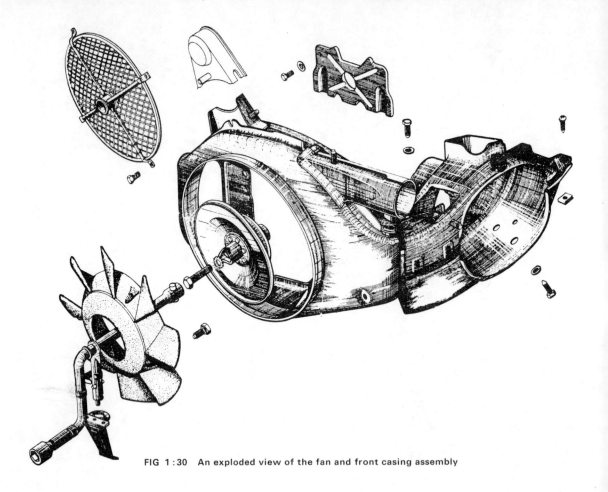

FIG 1:30 An exploded view of the fan and front casing assembly

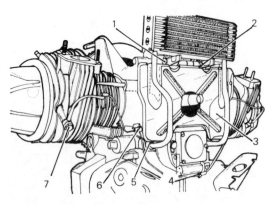

FIG 1:31 Oil cooler assembly

Key to Fig 1:31   1 Attaching screws to crankcase
2 Cross-pieces 3 Cover 4 Clamp 5 Unions securing the
pipes   6 Union attachment to crankcase   7 Union attachment to cylinder head

facilities and experience at the disposal of a service workshop. Examine the pilot bearing or bush in the end of the
crankshaft for wear. Renew if required as described in
Chapter 4. Use new bolts when refitting the flywheel
and tighten to a torque of 3.8 kg m, holding the flywheel
with a screwdriver through one of the holes in the
circumference.

From November 1972 the flywheel retaining bolts are
identified by three concentric circles on the head. These
should be tightened to a torque of 4.2 to 4.5 kg m.

To refit the clutch assembly, centre the disc by means
of a suitable mandrel. Ensure that the mandrel slides freely
when tightening the securing bolts and finally remove it.
If the appropriate mandrel is not available an old primary
shaft may be used.

1:7 Removing fan, oil cooler and oil pump

Access to the oil pump, camshaft and crankshaft
necessitates the separation of the crankcase halves,
which itself involves firstly the removal of the ancillary
assemblies followed by the dismantling of the main engine
components. The fan, oil cooler and oil pump are dealt
with in this Section as part of the lubrication system and

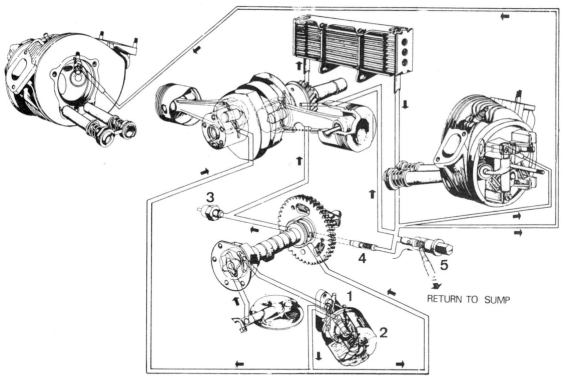

FIG 1:32 A diagrammatic view of the lubrication system

Key to Fig 1:32 1 Filter 2 Bypass valve 3 Pressure connection 4 Bypass valve in righthand half-housing 5 Relief valve

work on the camshaft and crankshaft is discussed in **Section 1:8**.

With the engine removed from the car, preliminary procedure is to drain the engine oil and rocker covers, then slacken the driving belt and remove the alternator (see **Section 1:4**), remove the fan protecting grille where applicable and the fan (see **FIG 1:30**). For the latter, a very thin walled tube spanner will be necessary to remove the centre fixing bolt. The fan assembly is a taper fit on the crankshaft and to free the joint it will be necessary to hold the flywheel with a screwdriver and give a sharp crank with the starting handle. If this method fails an extractor tool No. 3006T is available. The centre bolt must be screwed back in and unscrewed two turns before using the extractor. Do not attempt to free the fan by striking the starter dog as this may bend the crankshaft.

Continue the removal of the assemblies of the fuel pump, air cleaner and carburetter (see **Chapter 2**), the air manifold and cooling casing, the inlet and exhaust manifolds (see **Section 1:4**), the clutch and flywheel (see **Section 1:6**) the crankcase breather 4 (see **FIG 1:14**) and the dipstick and tube 5.

Referring to **FIG 1:31**, remove the retaining bolts 1, the two union nuts 5 attaching the pipes and withdraw the oil cooler with the two cross-pieces 2. Detach the cover 3, then remove the lubrication pipes to the cylinder heads by unscrewing the unions 6 and 7 and the retaining collar 4. A diagrammatic view of the lubrication system

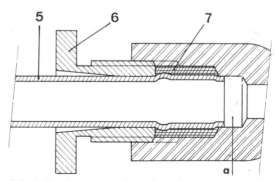

FIG 1:33 A sectional view of an oil cooler connecting pipe assembly

Key to Fig 1:33 a Recess 5 Pipe 6 Union 7 Seal

which includes the external oil filter, introduced from November 1970, is shown in **FIG 1:32**. As the oil cooler is part of the oil circulation system the engine must never be run without the cooler in position. It can be replaced by a tube, however, as a temporary expedient.

Before refitting the cooler it should be thoroughly cleaned. The recommended method is first to wash through the piping with kerosene and blow out with compressed air, then immerse the assembly in a bath of cellulose

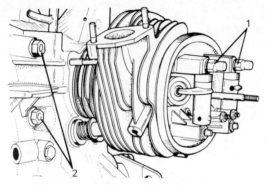

FIG 1:34   Crankcase and cylinder assembly

Key to Fig 1:34   1 Cylinder retaining nuts (lower nut not shown)   2 Half casing retaining bolts

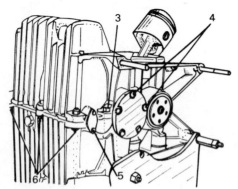

FIG 1:35   Positioning the crankcase for separation of the sections

Key to Fig 1:35   3 Retaining bolts   4 Oil pump cover bolts   5 Oil strainer flange bolts   6 Retaining bolts

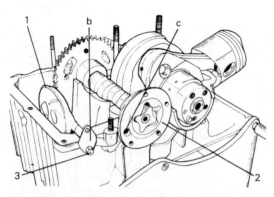

FIG 1:36   A view of the camshaft and crankshaft assembled in the half crankcase

Key to Fig 1:36   1 Oil strainer   2 Camshaft and oil pump   3 Flange bolt   b Oil strainer flange   c Lubrication hole aligned with similar hole in crankcase

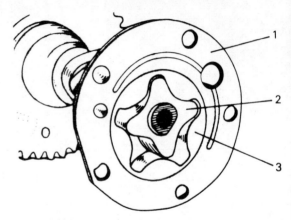

FIG 1:37   Oil pump, showing the body 1 and rotors 2 and 3

solvent for about half an hour and pour the thinner through the piping to remove all dirt, finally again blowing out with compressed air. Refitting is by reversing the removal operations, fitting new seals and washers.

If a big-end should seize up, showing ineffective lubrication, the oil cooler and strainer should be renewed, as well as making sure all oilways are clear and checking the operation of the oil pump, the pressure relief valve and the external oil filter if fitted. The new cooler should be cleaned out with petrol and dried out with compressed air before positioning it in front of the half-casing cover. Locate the ends of the connecting pipes in the casing, making sure the ends enter the recesses at 'a' (see **FIG 1:33**). Fit the unions 6 and tighten moderately to a torque of 1 to 2 kg m, noting that a new seal 7 must be used and set back 2 mm from the end of the tube. Locate the cross-pieces and fit the retaining bolts with flat washers under the heads and serrated washers under the nuts.

The dismantling of the engine proceeds with the removal of the cylinder heads, cylinders and associated components (see **Sections 1:4** and **1:5**) and the distributor (see **Chapter 3**). The cylinder head studs may be removed if required, using a tool No. 2410.T. Remove the four nuts 2 (see **FIG 1:34**) from the engine assembly and place it as shown in **FIG 1:35**, with the righthand half crankcase towards the bottom. Remove the bolts 4 and disengage the oil pump cover, also the upper bolt at 5 retaining the flange of the oil strainer.

The two sections of the crankcase may now be separated by removing the nuts and bolts retaining the assembly at 3 and 6. Place the pistons at TDC and disengage the top half of the crankcase, leaving the assembly shown in **FIG 1:36**. Remove the tappets from both sections. Proceed to remove (a) the oil strainer 1 (b) the camshaft with the oil pump 2 (c) the crankshaft assembly complete with connecting rods and pistons and front and rear oil seals.

If required, remove the oil pressure relief valve with piston and spring from the righthand section, the oil gallery plug on the lefthand section and the drain plug.

Disengage from the camshaft the pump body 1 (see **FIG 1:37**) and the rotors 2 and 3. Check the end

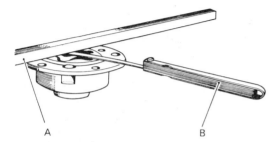

FIG 1:38 Checking oil pump rotor clearance with straightedge A and feeler gauges B

clearance of the rotors with a straightedge and feeler gauges as shown in **FIG 1:38**, when the clearance should be not more than .1 mm. Different types of pump bodies have been used before and after October, 1968. The earlier design and its location on the crankcase are shown in **FIG 1:39** and the later ones in **FIG 1:40**, the main differences being in the lubrication channels at a, b, c and d. A paper gasket is fitted dry between the flange and crankcase in the earlier assemblies and in the later ones the pump body is located on the crankcase with a sealer compound. Pump bodies of one type should never be assembled to crankcases designed for the other type, otherwise lubrication will be affected.

The internal oil filter shown in **FIG 1:41** need only be cleaned and fitted with a new oil seal 4 before reassembly. The seal is passed over the flange 'b'. Jointing compound is only used with the type of filter that does not incorporate an oil seal. It should be noted that as the crankcase of this type is not suitably reamed an oil seal cannot be fitted.

Some later vehicles have a renewable cartridge in the filter which must be changed whenever the engine is dismantled. Fit the lower retaining nut and washer 3 (see **FIG 1:36**), then refit the oil pump in the reverse manner of its removal. Smear the circumference of the inside face of the cover with jointing compound, applying sparingly so that on tightening, the compound will not be forced into the pump. Lubricate the rotors, attach the cover and tighten the bolts and washers to a torque of 13 kg m.

In addition to the internal oil strainer, some models are also fitted with an external filter of the disposable cartridge type. This is mounted low down at the rear of the engine on the righthand side.

A specially shaped ring tool is available for the removal of the filter cartridge, but any suitable strap type wrench should be satisfactory if it cannot be unscrewed by hand.

The new cartridge, required every 6000 miles, should be screwed into its mounting until it just contacts the seal face and then a further three-quarters of a turn by hand only.

1:8 Removing and refitting camshaft and crankshaft

Remove the camshaft (see **FIG 1:36**) complete with oil pump, timing gear wheel, distributor cam and advance weights (see **FIG 1:42**). The timing gear wheel is rigidly attached to the camshaft during manufacture and

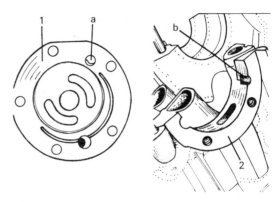

FIG 1:39 Oil pump body and lubrication before October, 1968

Key to Fig 1:39   1 Pump body   2 Crankcase face
a, b Lubrication holes

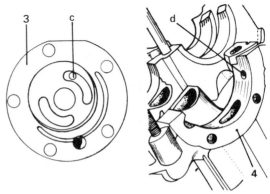

FIG 1:40 Oil pump body and lubrication after October, 1968

Key to Fig 1:40   3 Pump body   4 Crankcase face
c, d Lubrication holes

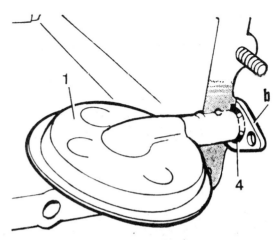

FIG 1:41 Fitting the oil strainer 1, showing the sealing ring 4 and the flange b

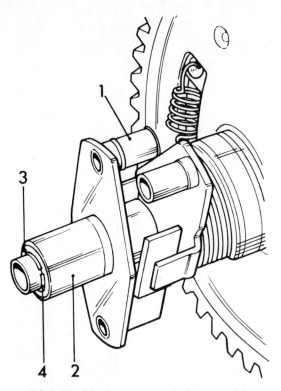

FIG 1 :42   Distributor cam and advance weights

Key to Fig 1 :42   1 Weights   2 Cam   3 Washer   4 Circlip

ing by 'Helicoil' inserts to allow the original studs to be used. If removed, refit the engine to gearbox studs, which have a 15 mm long screw thread on the ends which are inserted into the housing. The total overall lengths of the upper studs are 87 mm on the lefthand side and 95 mm on the righthand side and of the lower studs 80 mm lefthand and 75 mm righthand. Ensure that the mating faces on the crankcase sections are clean and that the locating dowels 2 (see **FIG 1 :45**) of the front and rear crankshaft bearings and of the camshaft bearing 1 are in position.

Lubricate the crankshaft bearings, place the rear bearing shell on the crankshaft journal and refit the crankshaft as shown in **FIG 1 :46**, so that the groove 'a' lies flush with the joint face at 'b'. Correctly engage the dowels in the front and rear bearings. Proceed to refit the oil strainer in the crankcase and the oil pump on the camshaft as described in **Section 1 :7**, also the distributor components at the other end of the camshaft if removed. Lubricate the camshaft bearings and locate the camshaft in the righthand half-casing, engaging the marks on the camshaft and crankshaft gears as shown in **FIG 1 :43** or **1 :47**. Reassemble the tappets.

is not detachable. As shown in **FIG 1 :43**, the gear consists of two toothed wheels of identical diameter linked together by springs, with the object of reducing backlash and wear. If excessive wear has occurred the camshaft must be renewed.

The distributor cam and weights are removed by detaching the circlip 4, the washer 3, the cam 2 and the weights 1. After removing the oil pump as described in the previous section, ensure that the camshaft is perfectly straight otherwise the points gap will not be the same on the two cam faces and the camshaft will have to be renewed. The camshaft runs in two bearings with nominal diameters of 36 mm and 20 mm for front and rear respectively. Thrust is taken on the front bearing.

The crankshaft is removed as the complete assembly shown in **FIG 1 :44**, and has two main bearings and two crankpins. The shaft cannot be reground and replacement bearing shells are not available. The specified diametrical clearance is .055 to .111 mm and the end play .07 to .14 mm. The end play is established by the fitting of the front bearing shell and is not adjustable. The front shell is retained behind the crankshaft pinion and is supplied assembled with the crankshaft, as are the connecting rods.

To refit the crankshaft and camshaft the half sections of the crankcase are prepared for reassembly. Inspect the condition of the stud screw threads in the half housings. If worn, the manufacturers recommend their recondition-

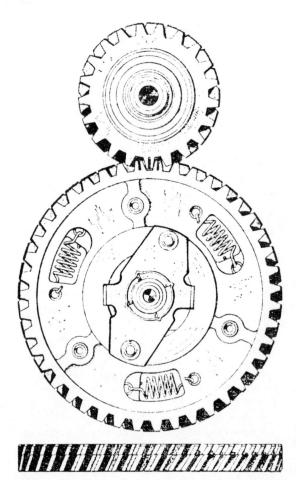

FIG 1 :43   Camshaft timing wheel showing the double gears

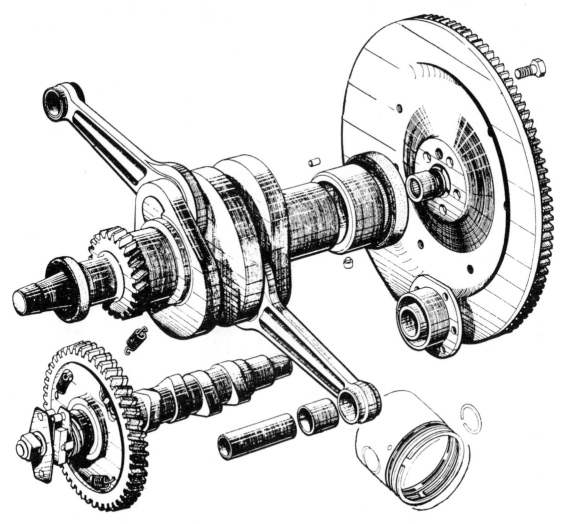

FIG 1:44 An exploded view of the camshaft and crankshaft

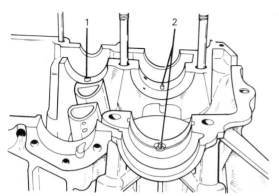

FIG 1:45 Crankcase half section showing bearing dowels **1** and **2**

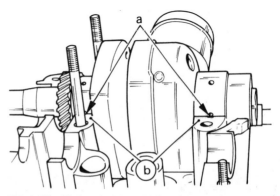

FIG 1:46 Fitting bearing shells with groove **a** flush with joint face **b**

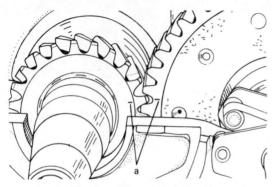

FIG 1:47 Markings to be aligned on crankshaft and camshaft timing gears

The oil seals must be changed whenever the engine is dismantled. Assemble the sealing rings on the crankshaft. For the front seal, smear the bore and the outer surface of the seal with high melting point grease and locate the ring with the face marked with the maker's name towards the outside of the engine. Insert the seal with the tool 3007.T shown in **FIG 1:48**, lubricating it with high melting point grease. The collar of the seal must be in contact with the chamfered edge machined inside the casing. A similar procedure is undertaken for the front

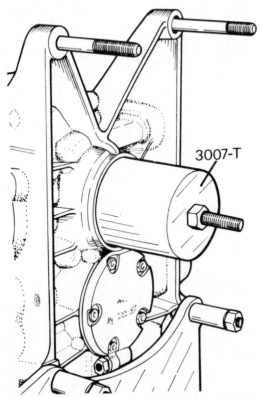

FIG 1:48 Fitting rear main bearing seal with the tool 3007.T

seal, inserting it with the aid of a tube of 31 mm inside diameter, 45 mm outside diameter and length of 100 mm. In each case take care not to damage the lips of the seals and particularly to fit them after fully tightening the crankcase sections, otherwise they may be caught up and oil leakage result.

Referring to **FIG 1:35**, coat the mating faces of the crankcase sections with sealing compound and assemble the lefthand section on the righthand one. Insert the second bolt of the oil strainer flange without tightening it, then tighten the five nuts and washers 6 to a torque of 1.9 kg m and the nut 3 to a torque of .3 to .5 kg m. Tighten the two oil strainer flange bolts to a torque of .5 kg m. Refit the cylinders, cylinder heads (see **Section 1:4** and **1:5**) and remaining assemblies in the reverse order of their removal.

1:9 Reassembling stripped engine

Much of the work of reassembling a stripped engine has already been described in previous sections, where it has been convenient to include it with other details concerning particular assemblies. The refitting of the crankshaft and camshaft has been described in **Section 1:8** and the oil pump and oil strainer in **Section 1:7**, followed by the reassembly of the crankcase described in **Section 1:8**. Fitting the oil cooler is described in **Section 1:7**, the cylinders and pistons in **Section 1:5**, the cylinder heads, rocker assemblies and valves in **Section 1:4**, the clutch and flywheel in **Section 1:6**, the distributor and ignition setting in **Chapter 3** and the carburetter and air cleaner in **Chapter 2**. Details of the operations concerned with the overhaul and reassembly of the generator and the starter motor are covered in **Chapter 11**. When refitting the fan, locate the generator belt then turn the engine to the firing point or TDC position. Assemble the fan so that the starting handle when fitted will be horizontal. Install the starting handle bracket and tighten the fan retaining screw and spring washer whilst holding the flywheel stationary.

1:10 Refitting engine in car

Take the weight of the engine and gearbox on suitable tackle and lower the unit into position. Clean and grease the sliding splines and engage the transmission. Assemble the handbrake cables to the locations in the crossmember. Rest the rear securing studs in the elongated rear mounting, fit the washers behind the mounting and continue to lower the unit whilst guiding the handbrake cable into the sockets on the swivel levers. Place the front mounting pad securing bolts in position and tighten them with locking washers under the heads. Procedure is then to follow the removal operations in reverse with attention to the following:

1 Reconnect all hoses, wiring harness and connections in the reverse order of their dismantling. Refit the accelerator linkage and the choke cable, leaving a clearance of 3 to 5 mm.
2 Fit the clutch linkage and make the required adjustments as described in **Chapter 4**. Secure the starter cable to the switch lever and adjust it so that it is neither tight nor slack. Refit the battery, connect up the terminals and check the ignition timing (see

Chapter 3). Check that the sparking plugs are clean and refit with gaps set as specified.

3 Refill the engine and transmission with the correct grade of lubricating oil according to the capacities given in **Technical Data**. After a final inspection to ensure that all components have been properly connected run the engine and carry out any minor adjustments which may be necessary, including attention to any oil leaks.

4 Final checks should be made on the oil pressure and crankcase depression, for which service agents possess the necessary adaptors and pressure and vacuum gauges. It is to be ensured that the oil filler cap and dipstick entry always make tight seals, as the depression in the crankcase reduces possibilities of oil leakage.

1 :11 Fault diagnosis

(a) Engine will not start

1 Defective coil
2 Faulty distributor capacitor
3 Dirty, pitted or incorrectly set contact breaker points
4 Ignition wires loose or insulation faulty
5 Water on sparking plug leads
6 Corrosion of battery terminals or discharged condition
7 Faulty or jammed starter
8 Sparking plug leads wrongly connected
9 Vapour lock in fuel pipes
10 Defective fuel pump
11 Overchoking
12 Underchoking
13 Blocked petrol filter or carburetter jets
14 Leaking valves
15 Sticking valves
16 Valve timing incorrect
17 Ignition timing incorrect

(b) Engine stalls

Check 1, 2, 3, 4, 10, 11, 12, 13, 14 and 15 in (a)
1 Sparking plugs defective or gap incorrect
2 Retarded ignition
3 Mixture too weak
4 Water in fuel system
5 Petrol tank breather choked
6 Incorrect valve clearance

(c) Engine idles badly

Check 1 and 6 in (b)
1 Air leak in manifold joints
2 Slow-running jet blocked or out of adjustment
3 Air leak in carburetter
4 Over-rich mixture

5 Worn piston rings
6 Worn valve stems or guides
7 Weak exhaust valve springs

(d) Engine misfires

Check 1, 2, 3, 4, 5, 8, 10, 13, 14, 15, 16 and 17 in (a) and 1, 2, 3 and 6 in (b)
1 Weak or broken valve springs

(e) Compression low

Check 14 and 15 in (a); 5 and 6 in (c) and 1 in (d)
1 Worn piston ring grooves
2 Scored or worn cylinder bores

(f) Engine lacks power

Check 3, 10, 11, 13, 14, 15 and 16 in (a); 1, 2, 3 and 6 in (b); 5 and 6 in (c) and 1 in (d). Also check (e)
1 Fouled spark plugs

(g) Burnt valves or seats

Check 14 and 15 in (a); 6 in (b) and 1 in (d). Also check (e)
1 Excessive carbon around valve seat and head

(h) Sticking valves

Check 1 in (d)
1 Bent valve stem
2 Scored valve stem, or guide
3 Incorrect valve clearance

(j) Excessive cylinder wear

Check 11 in (a) and check (c)
1 Lack of oil
2 Dirty oil
3 Piston rings gummed up or broken
4 Badly fitting piston rings
5 Connecting rods bent

(k) Excessive oil consumption

Check 5 and 6 in (c) and check (j)
1 Ring gaps too wide
2 Scored cylinders
3 Oil level too high
4 External oil leaks

(l) Crankshaft and connecting rod failure

Check 1 in (j)
1 Restricted oilways
2 Worn journals or crankpins
3 Extremely low oil pressure
4 Bent connecting rod

(m) High fuel consumption (see **Chapter 2**)

NOTES

CHAPTER 2

THE FUEL SYSTEM

2 : 1 Description

Fuel is supplied from a tank which has a capacity according to the model concerned, i.e. 25 litre on the Ami 6, 31 litre on the Ami 8, 20 litre on the 2CV and Dyane 4 and 25 litre on the Dyane 6. From the tank the fuel is carried by a pipe connected to an SEV or Guiot type mechanical fuel pump (see **FIGS 2 : 1** and **2 : 2**) mounted on the lefthand side of the crankcase. The action of the pump is that a rocker arm or lever is given a reciprocating movement and operates a flexible diaphragm against a spring to create a partial vacuum in the pump, which enables the atmospheric pressure in the tank to send fuel through the connecting pipe to the pump. The return action of the spring then pushes the diaphragm upwards to deliver the fuel to the carburetter float chamber. When the bowl is full the float closes a needle valve, preventing further supply from the pump until the carburetter requires more fuel and the needle valve opens. In the meantime the pump rocker arm is given an idling movement.

The Ami 8, later Ami 6, most Dyane 6 and post-1978 2CV6 models are fitted with the Solex 26/35 downdraught double-barrel carburetter. From 1978, a cable-controlled throttle with pendant pedal has been fitted to Dyanes. Other vehicles are fitted with a single-barrel carburetter, the type of which will be found in the vehicle identification chart at the end of this manual. The single-barrel carburettters fitted to the A53 engine are of similar design to those used on later cars. The asterisks denote the carburetters used with vehicles having a conventional clutch.

The alternative types of carburetter used in cars fitted with the optional centrifugal clutch (see **Chapter 4**) incorporate a deceleration delay device. This takes the form of a dashpot arrangement connected to the throttle flap in the first or single barrel which has the effect of retarding the rate of decrease of engine speed when the car slows down and prevents a premature disengagement of the centrifugal clutch. Adjustments of the two types of carburetter are otherwise similar.

2 : 2 Fuel pump maintenance

Action of the pumps is automatic and normally no maintenance is required. If trouble is experienced with the fuel supply the first approach should be to ensure that there are no leaks or obstructions in the fuel line. Should the pump then become suspect, a quick check can be made by disconnecting the pipe at the pump outlet and turning the engine by the starter motor, when fuel should spurt from the outlet. Another test is to disconnect the inlet union and hold a finger over it whilst again turning

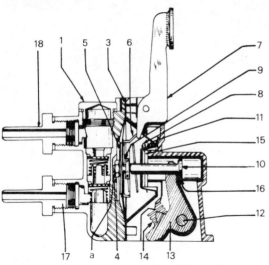

FIG 2:1 A sectional view of the Guiot fuel pump

Key to Fig 2:1 1 Plug 3 Assembly of three diaphragms 4 Nut 5 Washer 6 Thrust cup 7 Priming lever 8 Diaphragm spring 9 Gasket 10 Pushrod 11 Spring cup 12 Operating lever shaft 13 Operating lever 14 Return spring 15 Washers 16 Split washer 17 Outlet 18 Inlet **a** End of pushrod

the engine by the starter motor, when suction should be felt. With the pump removed from the engine it can be tested for leaks by closing the outlet to the carburetter with a plug, fitting a rubber hose on the inlet opening and immersing the whole pump in a container filled with clean petrol. Compressed air is then blown through the rubber hose at a pressure of $1\frac{1}{2}$ to $4\frac{1}{2}$ lb/sq in (.1 to .3 kg/sq cm), when bubbles of escaping air will indicate either a defective diaphragm or leaking gaskets.

2:3 Fuel pump servicing

To remove a fuel pump it is necessary first to disconnect the battery negative cable, then remove the lefthand side sparking plug and the air silencer with fittings as described in **Chapter 1**. Disconnect the flexible pipes from the inlet and outlet of the pump, which can then be withdrawn after removing the two retaining nuts. Disengage the spacer, clean it and remove the operating spindle.

In Guiot pumps (see **FIG 2:1**) disengage the upper part of the pump from the body and remove the diaphragms retaining nut. Withdraw the round washer, the assembly of three diaphragms, the thrust cup, the return spring and the cup washer. Continue to remove the pushrod from the operating lever, the two round washers and the split washer. Clean and examine the parts for wear, renewing any that appear unserviceable. The inlet

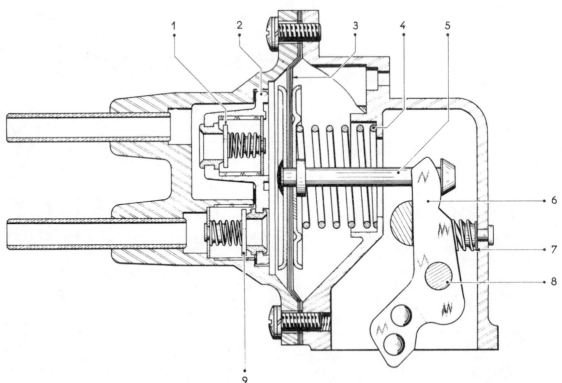

FIG 2:2 A sectional view of the SEV fuel pump

Key to Fig 2:2 1 Inlet valve 2 Valve holder 3 Diaphragm assembly 4 Diaphragm spring 5 Pushrod 6 Operating lever 7 Return spring 8 Lever spindle 9 Outlet valve

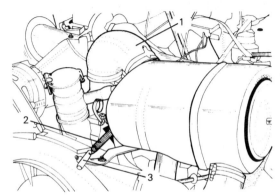

FIG 2:3 Carburetters controls, showing: **1** Connecting hose, **2** Accelerator spring, **3** Deceleration adjuster

and outlet valves are not detachable and if defective the renewal of the upper body assembly will be necessary. Refit the components in the reverse order of their disassembly, noting that the diaphragms must be in good condition and fitted completely dry. Fit and tighten all nuts removed and hold the pushrod with pliers to prevent it turning.

Operations are similar in SEV pumps (see **FIG 2:2**), allowing for design differences in construction. Note that care must be taken to ensure that the diaphragm pushrod assembly is correctly engaged in the operating lever fork. Inlet and outlet valves are also not individually renewable.

To refit the pumps, lubricate the spindle and ensure that it turns freely in the bore. Turn the engine to bring the operating rod into its lowest position, then refit the spacer after ensuring that its mating faces are quite clean. Check that the operating rod protrudes at least 1.2 mm from the outer face of the spacer. Also check the length of the rod, which should be between 110.6 and 110.7 mm. If necessary either reduce the thickness of the spacer or otherwise renew it. Fill the location of the rod in the spacer with grease. Then offer up the pump to the crankcase and fit and tighten the two retaining nuts. Refit the items removed for access in the reverse order of their disassembly.

2:4 Removing and refitting carburetter

To remove a carburetter, detach the air filter or manifold (see **Chapter 1**) as necessary according to model. Proceed as follows:

1 Disconnect the battery negative cable, the connecting hose 1 (see **FIG 2:3**) and the fuel inlet on the carburetter.
2 Disconnect the retaining nut or screw 3 and slacken the sleeve 1 (see **FIG 2:6**) securing the choke control.
3 Remove the spring 2 (shown at 9 in **FIG 2:4**) and its tension adjuster 3, noting the position of the latter. Referring to **FIG 2:4**, remove the assembly 10, 8 and 7 from the throttle control.
4 Remove the retaining nuts on the manifolds, disengage the support 5 and withdraw the carburetter and spacer. Plug the manifold opening(s) to avoid entry of foreign matter whilst the carburetter is absent.

5 When refitting the carburetter, coat each side of the spacer 2 (see **FIG 2:5**). For double-barrelled carburetters the holes in the spacer must correspond with those in the carburetter, the hole with the smaller diameter and the corner 'a' being located towards the front of the engine. In some engines the carburetter is installed with a paper joint and in these cases the manufacturers recommend that the paper joint should be replaced by a spacer No. 124-98C with front studs 1 No. 818.S and rear studs 3 820.S.
6 Continue operations in the reverse order of those undertaken for removal. Refit the spring 2 (see **FIG 2:3**) with its adjuster 3 as originally set.
7 Adjust the throttle control by means of a 4 mm spacer under the accelerator pedal so that there is not more than 1.5 mm between the pin 7 (see **FIG 2:4**) and the end of the cable 4. If necessary a further adjustment may be made on the sleeve 2 shown in **FIG 2:6**.
8 After refitting the remaining items, adjust the slow-running as described in **Section 2:7**. If a centrifugal clutch is used, check the adjustment of the retainer 3 shown in **FIG 2:3** for a deceleration delay of one to two seconds.

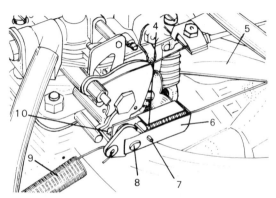

FIG 2:4 Carburetter controls

Key to Fig 2:4 **4** End of cable **5** Support **6** Throttle control spring **7** Pin **8** Spindle **9** Spring **10** Stop pin

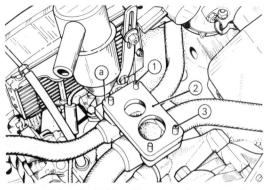

FIG 2:5 Manifolds with carburetter removed

Key to Fig 2:5 **1/3** Studs **2** Spacer **a** Corner at front of engine

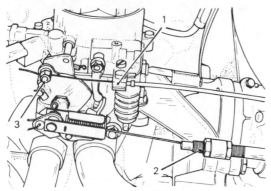

FIG 2:6 Carburetter details, showing: 1 Choke control sleeve, 2 Adjusting sleeve, 3 Retaining nut

2:5 Solex 26/35 SCIC and CSIC

Diagrams showing the operation of the Solex 26/35 carburetter are given in **FIG 2:7** and an exploded view of its components in **FIG 2:8**. Referring to **FIG 2:7**, the main jets 5 are situated at the bottom of the float chamber and the mixture is automatically adjusted by the compensator jets 1 incorporated in the emulsion tubes. The two throttle flaps 15 and 16 are mechanically interconnected so that the flap in the second barrel only opens when that in the first barrel is already about two-thirds open, which provides for smooth running and optimum fuel consumption. Calibrated air bleeds are provided at 13 into the carburetter main air inlet and at 14 into the narrowest part of the choke tube. At slow-running or idling speed the throttle flap in the first barrel is practically closed and simultaneously fuel is drawn through the slow-running jet 6. The resultant mixture is drawn through a drilling to a discharge hole controlled by the mixture volume control screw 18 into the carburetter barrel bore where, together with the air bleeding past the throttle flap, it forms a combustible mixture. The volume of air past the throttle flap is controlled by the setting of the throttle stop screw. The flow of fuel is controlled by the

size of the jet, the degree of depression allowed and the mixture volume control screw setting.

During idling, with the throttle flap closed, the accelerator pump diaphragm 11 is held by a spring which allows fuel to enter the pump chamber. Two levers connect the diaphragm to the accelerator and are interconnected by a spring and a cam on the first barrel throttle flap shaft. When the accelerator is depressed the throttle flap opens and the movement of the shaft causes the diaphragm to discharge fuel through the pump injector 9.

The econostat system has not been fitted since December, 1968. As shown, however, it consists mainly of a discharge tube 3 which takes fuel from the float chamber into the main air duct in the carburetter second barrel. Action is controlled by the rate of air flow and the device only operates at high engine speeds, to give the correct mixture whilst a minimum flow is provided at low engine speeds.

The choke flap facilitates starting under cold conditions and also assists idling when the engine is cold and during the warming up period. It has a cable operated control which is designed by means of a system of levers, cams and springs to return the control on release to an intermediate position corresponding to the partial opening of the choke flap and the first barrel throttle flap.

An exploded view showing the separate parts of the carburetter is given in **FIG 2:8**. To dismantle it for cleaning and inspection, first remove the six screws 1 (see **FIG 2:9**) to disengage the upper section of the float chamber. Proceed as follows, referring to **FIGS 2:9**, **2:10** and **2:11**.

1 Remove the spindle 9 and the float assembly 8, the pointed screw 10 with its spring 11 and its copper washer, the two paper gaskets 7 and the filter and plug 6.

2 On centrifugal clutch models remove the lever 3 and its stop 12, the piston rod 20 and the piston and spring assembly 21.

3 Withdraw the main jets 22 and 17 from each barrel, the pump injector 15, the air compensating orifices 13 and 18, the slow-running jet 14, the econostat 19

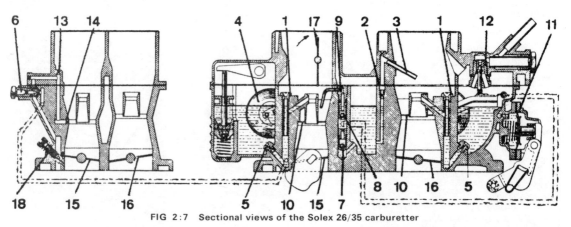

FIG 2:7 Sectional views of the Solex 26/35 carburetter

Key to Fig 2:7   1 Compensator jets   2 Econostat metering orifice   3 Econostat discharge tube   4 Floats   5 Main jets
6 Idling jet   7 and 8 Ball seats   9 Pump injector   10 Discharge nozzles   11 Pump diaphragm   12 Valve
13 and 14 Metering orifices   15 and 16 Throttle flaps   17 Choke flap   18 Mixture screw

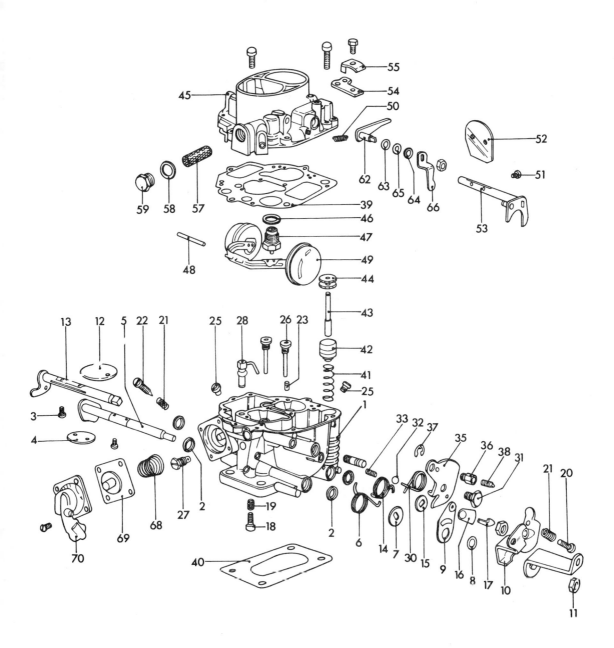

FIG 2:8   An exploded view of the Solex 26/35 carburetter

Key to Fig 2:8   1 Body and float chamber   2 Joint rings   3 Screw   4 Throttle flap   5 Throttle flap spindle and pump cam
6 Return spring   7 Washer   8 Spacer ring   9 Control lever, second barrel   10 Control lever   11 Nut   12 Throttle flap
13 Spindle   14 Return spring   15 Washer   16 Intermediate lever and bush   17 Link   18 Stop screw   19 Spring   20 Idling screw
21 Spring   22 Mixture screw   23 Econostat jet, second barrel   25 Main jet   26 Emulsion tube   27 Idling jet   28 Pump injector
30 Intermediate lever spring   31 Intermediate lever spindle   32 Locking ball   33 Spring   35 Intermediate lever   36 Nut
37 Circlip   38 Cable clamp screw   39 Float chamber gasket   40 Flange gasket   41 Dashpot spring   42 Dashpot piston   43 Plunger
44 Locating rings   45 Float chamber upper section   46 Needle valve joint   47 Needle valve   48 Float pivot pin   49 Floats
50 Spring   51 Screw   52 Choke flap   53 Choke spindle   54 Cable support   55 Clamp   57 Filter   58 Washer   59 Plug
62 Dashpot stop lever   63 Cup washer   64 Washer   65 Washer   66 Operating lever   68 Pump spring   69 Diaphragm assembly
70 Pump cover assembly

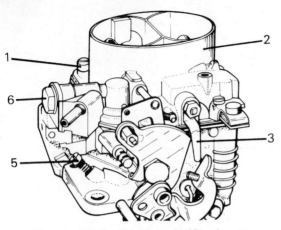

FIG 2:9   Details of the Solex 26/35 carburetter

Key to Fig 2:9   1 Securing screws   2 Upper section
3 Deceleration lever   5 Mixture screw   6 Filter plug

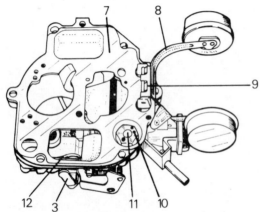

FIG 2:10   Details of the Solex 26/35 carburetter

Key to Fig 2:10   3 Deceleration lever   7 Paper gaskets
8 Float assembly   9 Spindle   10 Pointed screw   11 Spring
12 Stop lever

(where fitted) and the mixture control screw and spring 5.

4 Remove the accelerator pump cover 16 together with the diaphragm and spring.

5 Clean all parts with petrol and check the jet sizes with those given in **Technical Data**. Ensure that all drillings and jet orifices are unobstructed and blow through them with compressed air. Never use wire or anything which may enlarge the orifices. Renew any parts which appear unserviceable, giving particular attention to the accelerator pump diaphragm if its condition is doubtful.

6 Reassemble the carburetter in the reverse order of the dismantling operations. On completion adjust the throttle stop screw 22 in **FIG 2:12**. With the flap closed, bring the head of the screw 22 into contact with the lever 23 and then unscrew it by a quarter to half a turn. Check that the flap opens without binding.

7 In vehicles with centrifugal clutches, ensure that the dashpot lever moves freely. Accelerate sharply and release the accelerator. Note the time taken between the moment at which the throttle flap lever contacts the dashpot lever and the moment at which the end of the stop screw contacts the choke control lever, which should be no more than 1 to 2 seconds. Select the adjusting rod notch (3 in **FIG 2:3**) necessary for this requirement.

2:6 Solex single choke carburetters

The single choke carburetters are of PCIS or PICS types according to the type of clutch fitted. Performances vary in relation to engine requirements and jet sizes and other controlling features, but in general their construction and operation are similar.

Referring to the sectional views of the 34 PICS 4 carburetter shown in **FIG 2:13**, fuel is supplied through the main jet C which is screwed obliquely into the bottom of the float chamber. An air compensator jet A provides the required mixture and the emulsion tube L is incorporated with the carburetter body. The operation of the accelerator pump diaphragm J and injector I follows the same procedure as described for the accelerator pump in the previous Section.

At idling speed fuel is supplied through the idling jet E. Engine speed is adjusted by the stop screw and the mixture by the screw Q. The emulsion air enters by a calibrated duct from the main carburetter inlet. Bypass holes in the emulsion tube L are designed so that as the throttle flap opens they successively release more fuel mixture to give a progressive transition from idling to normal main jet running. The bypass system receives fuel through the jet D and air through the calibrated orifice N by way of the carburetter main inlet.

When the engine is started from cold, the choke knob is pulled and held out and the choke flap closed. As the engine starts, the depression created causes the choke flap to open slightly for the correct amount of mixture to be delivered to avoid stalling. With the choke knob

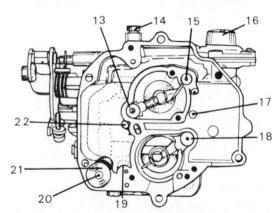

FIG 2:11   Details of the Solex 26/35 carburetter

Key to Fig 2:11   13 Calibrated air bleed   14 Slow-running
jet   15 Pump injector   16 Pump cover   17 Main jet,
secondary body   18 Calibrated air bleed   19 Econostat
20 Deceleration piston pushrod   21 Centring washer
22 Main jet, primary body

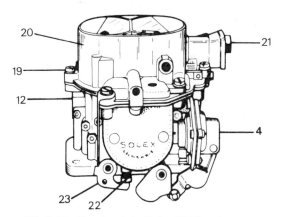

FIG 2:12 Details of the Solex 26/35 carburetter

Key to Fig 2:12   4 Pump cover   12 Paper gaskets
19 Retaining nuts   20 Upper section   21 Filter plug and
copper washer   22 Stop screw   23 Stop lever

released, the spring 49 (see **FIG 2:14**) acts on the choke flap and together with the cam on the lever 48 produces a fast idle condition for warming up. On the engine reaching its operating temperature the choke knob is fully pushed in, completely opening the choke flap for normal running.

Dismantling operations for a 32 PCIS carburetter are as follows:

1 Referring to **FIGS 2:15, 2:16** and **2:17**, detach the upper part of the float chamber and the paper gasket 3.

2 Remove the filter plug 1 and the filter, the pointed screw and copper washer 13, the slow-running lever 9 and its stop lever 11, the choke flap 12 and its spindle 'a' and spring.

3 Remove the float 22, its spindle 21, the piston rod 24 of the deceleration device, the centring washer 23, the piston and the spring.

4 Remove the slow-running jet 20, the main jet 14, the non-return valve 15 and the nozzle 16.

5 Remove the choke lever 19 and its spring. Remove the nut 18 and detach the lever 6 from the throttle flap spindle 17.

6 Remove the accelerator pump cover and then the pump diaphragm and spring. Do not unscrew the nut 5 which regulates the pump delivery rate.

7 Remove the throttle lever 8, the throttle flap and its spindle. Remove the mixture screw 7 and its spring.

Overhaul procedure is undertaken as described in Operation 5 in **Section 2:5**. Reassemble the components in the reverse order of their removal, renewing any which appear unserviceable. Do not tighten the mixture screw to avoid englarging the hole or damaging the thread. Adjust the slow running on completion (see **Section 2:7**).

2:7 Adjusting for slow running

On twin choke carburetters the engine should be at normal operating temperature. Bring the engine speed to 750 rev/min by means of the throttle stop screw and then slowly screw in the mixture screw until the engine starts to hunt, on the point of stalling. Unscrew the mixture screw by about one-third of a turn to produce the correct mixture. Reset the throttle stop screw to give an idling speed of between 750 and 800 rev/min. If a centrifugal clutch is fitted slowly screw in the stop screw until the clutch drum just begins to turn, then unscrew the stop screw by one-eighth of a turn.

On single-choke carburetters, first fully release the throttle stop screw, then put the choke lever in the closed position. Adjust the throttle lever fully to close the throttle flap, tighten the stop screw to bring its end into contact with the lever and then tighten again two turns. Fully screw in the mixture screw without excessively tightening it, then unscrew by two turns. Proceed with the adjustments for slow-running as described for the twin choke carburetters. The correct idling speeds are given in **Technical Data**.

2:8 Renewing an exhaust silencer

Operations to renew an exhaust silencer are as follows:

1 Except on vans, remove the spare wheel. On van models remove the side panel and the front righthand wing should be removed.

2 Remove the clamps securing the silencer to the exhaust pipe and to the heat exchangers, then loosen the bolts retaining the silencer to the gearbox housing.

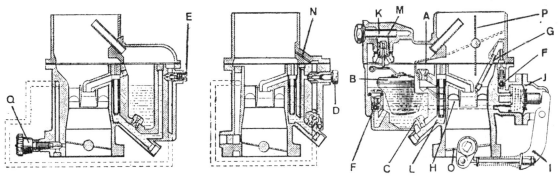

FIG 2:13 Sectional views of the Solex 34 carburetter

Key to Fig 2:13   A Air compensator jet   B Float   C Main jet   D Bypass jet   E Idling jet   F Ball   G Pump injector
H Diffusion orifice   I Pump lever   J Diaphragm   K Pointed screw   L Emulsion tube   M Filter   N Calibrated orifice   O Throttle
flap   P Choke flap   Q Idling mixture screw

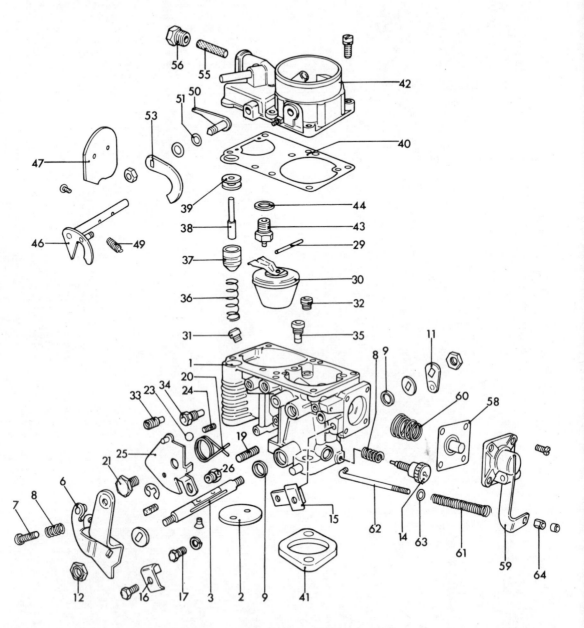

FIG 2:14 An exploded view of the Solex 34 carburetter

Key to Fig 2:14 1 Float chamber 2 Throttle flap 3 Spindle 6 Throttle lever 7 Idling stop screw 8 Spring 9 Washer 11 Pump intermediate lever 14 Mixture screw 15 Cable support 16 Clamp 19 Spring 20 Lever spring 21 Lever screw 23 Locking ball 24 Spring 25 Flap lever 26 Clamp screw 29 Float pivot pin 30 Float 31 Main jet 32 Air compensating jet 33 Idling jet 34 Bypass jet 35 Ball seat and 'O' ring 36 Damper spring 37 Damper piston 38 Plunger 39 Locating bush 40 Gasket 41 Spacer 42 Float chamber cover 43 Needle valve assembly 44 Washer 47 Choke flap 48 Spindle and cam 49 Return spring 50 Dashpot stop lever 51 Cup washer 53 Dashpot operating lever 55 Filter 56 Plug 58 Pump diaphragm assembly 59 Pump cover and lever 60 Diaphragm spring 61 Pump link spring 62 Operating link 63 Stop washer 64 Adjusting nut

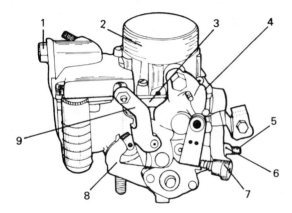

FIG 2:15   Details of the Solex 32 carburetter

Key to Fig 2:15   1 Filter plug   2 Carburetter upper section
3 Paper gasket   4 Linkage   5 Adjusting screw   6 Lever
7 Mixture screw   8 Throttle lever   9 Slow running lever

3 Withdraw the silencer from under the vehicle and fit the new unit in the reverse order of the removal operations. Ensure that the clutch cable is securely retained in its clip and not in contact with the silencer.
4 Refit the items removed for access.

2:9 Air cleaner

Air cleaners fitted are of Lautrette or Miofiltre manufacture and are of different design according to vehicle model and date of manufacture. All, however, are attached to the carburetter air inlet by a flexible clip and have the common feature of an oil-wetted type element.

The filter element is exposed as shown at 2 in **FIG 2:18** after removing the central retaining wing-nut and the cover of the air cleaner. Withdraw the element and clean it with petrol, cleaning the interior of the housing at the same time. Dip the element in engine oil and allow it to drain, then insert it into its casing and refit the cover.

2:10 Emission control carburetters

Solex carburetters of the type 26/35 SCIC or CSIC are fitted to 1973 models of the Dyane 6 and Ami 8 in the interests of reduced exhaust gas pollution. They are very similar to the earlier carburetters, but use a different method of regulating the idle fuel supply as may be seen from reference to **FIG 2:18** and the following description.

The idle jet 6 supplies the fuel while the associated air supply is metered through a channel opening into the main air duct of the carburetter 13.

A screw 19 fitted in the body, as shown, takes the place of the throttle stop screw and regulates the air supply through a channel opening into the main air duct below the throttle valves to be added to the idle mixture, thus controlling the idle speed of the engine. Adjustment of the fuel mixture is by means of the mixture control screw 18.

Idle adjustment:

Do not attempt to use the throttle stop screws as these are pre-set at the factory.

Bring the engine up to normal working temperature and check that the throttle is completely closed.

Use the idle air screw 19 to bring the engine speed to 750 to 800 rev/min and then, by means of the mixture control screw 18 adjust the mixture strength to give a CO reading of .8 to 1.6 per cent and a CO_2 content of 9 to 12.5 per cent. These values must be obtained while holding the engine speed to the specified figure, with an ambient temperature between 15° and 30°C.

On vehicles fitted with a centrifugal clutch, open the throttle wide and then release the accelerator pedal. Note carefully the time elapsing between the throttle control lever contacting the dashpot lever and the moment when the end of the stop screw touches the cam on the choke control lever. This time interval must be between 1 and 2 seconds. Any adjustment necessary may be made by selecting the appropriate notch on the control lever on

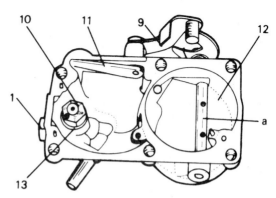

FIG 2:16   Details of the Solex 32 carburetter

Key to Fig 2:16   1 Filter plug   9 Slow-running lever
10 Nut and copper washer   11 Stop lever   12 Choke flap
and spindle (a)   13 Pointed screw

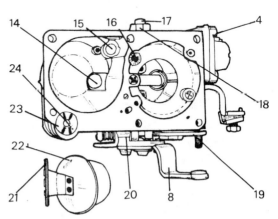

FIG 2:17   Details of the Solex 32 carburetter

Key to Fig 2:17   4 Pump cover   8 Throttle lever
14 Main jet   15 Non-return valve   16 Nozzle   17 Spindle
18 Nut   19 Choke lever   20 Slow-running jet   21 Spindle
22 Float   23 Centring washer   24 Piston rod

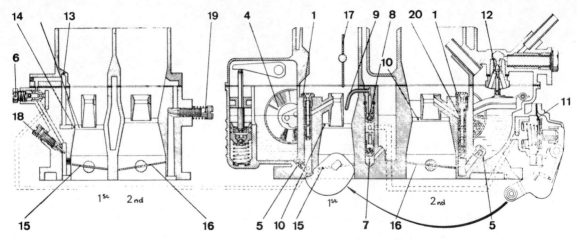

FIG 2:18 Sectional views of Solex carburetter 26/35 since 1973

Key to Fig 2:18   1 Compensating jets   4 Float   5 Main jets   6 Idle jet   7, 8 Ball valves   9 Pump injector   10 Diffusers
11 Diaphragm   12 Needle and spring   13, 14 Calibrated holes   15, 16 Throttles   17 Choke   18 Idle mixture control screw
19 Idle air screw   20 Emulsion tubes

the air cleaner. Note that the spring should be stretched
to reduce the time and vice versa.

Adjustment of single choke carburetters is carried out
by following the above procedure, but the idle speed may
be between 750 and 850 rev/min.

2:11 Fault diagnosis

(a) Insufficient or no fuel delivered

1 Carburetter float needle stuck
2 Pressure failure on fuel pump
3 Fuel feed pipes blocked
4 Air leaks in pipe connections
5 Pump diaphragm or gaskets defective
6 Pump valves sticking or seating badly
7 Fuel tank air vent restricted or blocked
8 Fuel vaporizing in feed pipes due to heat
9 Pump or carburetter filters blocked

(b) Difficult cold start

1 Insufficient fuel, see (a)
2 Needle valve sticking
3 Choke plate not closing properly
4 Incorrect throttle opening on choke operation

(c) Difficult warm start

1 Over-rich mixture
2 Unserviceable air cleaner
3 Pump pressure high
4 Needle valve seating loose or dirty
5 Float punctured or float arm bent

(d) Excessive fuel consumption

1 Carburetter needs adjustment
2 Choke opening impeded
3 Dirty air cleaner
4 Idling speed too high
5 Incorrect pump linkage setting
6 Fuel leakage
7 Brakes binding
8 Tyres under-inflated
9 Excessive engine temperature
10 Car overloaded

(e) Stalling and irregular slow-running

1 Volume and idling screws need adjusting
2 Volume control screw spring unserviceable
3 Idling jet dirty

(f) Idling speed too high

1 Slow-running screw needs adjusting
2 Over-rich fuel mixture
3 Carburetter controls sticking
4 Choke plate unserviceable or needs adjusting

(g) Poor acceleration

1 Accelerator pump jet dirty
2 Piston and ball valve need cleaning

(h) Noisy fuel pump

1 Loose mountings
2 Air leaks on suction side and at diaphragm
3 Obstruction in fuel pipe
4 Clogged pump filter

CHAPTER 3

THE IGNITION SYSTEM

3:1 Operating principles of automatic timing controls

The main elements in the ignition system providing high-tension current to the sparking plugs are the battery, the ignition coil, the contact breaker and the automatic advance mechanism. The moving parts are mounted on the end of the camshaft behind the cooling fan and consist of two main assemblies. As shown in **FIG 1:42** in **Chapter 1**, a cam and centrifugal weights are individually located on the camshaft. Superimposed over the cam is the ignition box or distributor, which contains the contact breaker mechanism and can be separately withdrawn. A capacitor, which absorbs the current flow at the time of the separation of the contact points and prevents sparking and burning, is fitted below the ignition box.

The cam has two lobes, one for each cylinder. Ignition advance is mechanically controlled by the governor weights moving outwards as the engine speed increases, rotating the cam and so advancing the point of ignition. The ignition coil delivers HT current to both sparking plugs at the same time, so that an effective firing spark is created at the top of the compression stroke in one cylinder at the same time as an ineffective spark occurs at the top of the exhaust stroke in the other cylinder.

3:2 Distributor maintenance, contact point adjustment

Maintenance requirements are chiefly concerned with occasional lubrication of the moving parts, which must be undertaken sparingly. The cam faces may be lightly smeared with petroleum jelly and if required only a film of engine oil may be applied to the breaker arm pivot. Care must be taken that no lubricant reaches the breaker points, resulting in burning and difficult starting.

Adjustment of the contact breaker points may be made either by measuring the cam angle or by using feeler gauges to measure the points separation. The cam angle or dwell angle represents the number of degrees the distributor cam rotates from the instant that the contact points close to the instant when they open again, which in current vehicles should be 109 ± 3 deg., corresponding to a points gap of $.4 \pm .05$ mm. A difference of no more than 1 deg. 30 min. should exist between the dwell angles of the two cam lobes. An oscilloscope or cam angle meter is necessary for this kind of measurement,

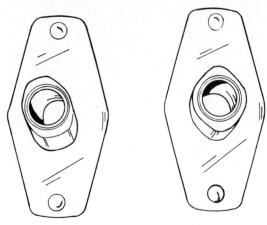

FIG 3:1 The cam as fitted to current vehicles (left) and pre-1970 vehicles (right)

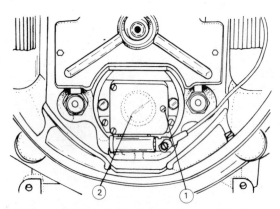

FIG 3:2 The ignition box cover 2 and the retaining screws 1

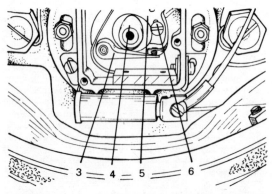

FIG 3:3 Contact breaker details showing the breaker arm 3, the cam 4, the fixed contact 5 and the retaining screw 6

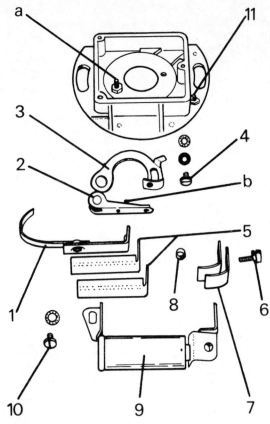

FIG 3:4 An exploded view of the ignition box or distributor

Key to Fig 3:4 1 Spring 2 Breaker arm 3 Fixed contact 4 Screw 5 Insulators 6 Brass screw 7 Insulators 8 Insulating washer 9 Capacitor 10 Screw 11 Backplate a Pivot b Fibre

however, which is normally to be undertaken by a service agent. It gives more accuracy than feeler gauges, which can measure only between high spots on the points.

Vehicles produced before February 1970 are fitted with the earlier type cam as shown in **FIG 3:1**. The dwell angle with this cam is 144 ± 2 deg.

A less exact adjustment may be obtained with feeler gauges as follows:

1 Remove the cooling fan and front grille as described in **Chapter 1**.
2 Referring to **FIG 3:2**, remove the screws 1 and detach the cover 2. Examine the contact points for wear. Contacts showing a greyish colour and which are only slightly pitted need not be renewed. If still serviceable, clean them with a fine contact stone. Do not use emery cloth or sandpaper. All roughness need not be removed, only scale and dirt. If the contact points are excessively burnt or pitted a new assembly should be fitted.
3 Referring to **FIG 3:3**, turn the engine by the flywheel so that one of the lobes of the cam 4 raises the breaker arm 3 to its maximum extent. Measure the points gap,

which should be .4 mm. If not, slacken the fixed contact screw 6 to adjust the fixed contact to give the required setting, then retighten the screw 6.

4 Now turn the engine so that the second cam lobe fully lifts the arm 3 and again measure the points gap. If the result is less than .35 mm or more than .45 mm either the ignition cam or the camshaft is unserviceable.

5 For further inspection remove the ignition box (see **Section 3:3**) without turning the engine. Withdraw the cam from the end of the camshaft, turn it through 180 deg. and refit it. Refit the ignition box and with the breaker arm at its highest level again measure the points gap.

6 If the result is between .35 and .45 mm it shows that the other lobe of the cam is worn and the cam must be renewed. If the result is the same as in Operation 4, the end of the camshaft is worn and the camshaft requires renewal (see **Chapter 1**).

7 Refit the items removed for access.

3:3 Distributor removal, servicing and refitting

Dismantling of the main assemblies is preceded by the removal of the fan, front grille and ignition box cover (see **Section 3:2**). Further operations are as follows:

1 Referring to **FIG 3:4**, remove the screws 6 and 10, the capacitor 9 with its brass terminal and the two insulating pieces 7.

2 Withdraw the contact breaker arm 2 from its pivot 'a' with the spring 1 and the two insulators 5.

3 Remove the screws 4 and the fixed contact 3. Take out the insulator 8 in the socket of the brass screw 6.

4 Remove the retaining bolts at each side (see **FIG 3:5**) to withdraw the housing 11.

5 Clean all the components and examine the condition of the contact points (see **Section 3:2**). Check the breaker arm spring tension with a small spring balance, which should show between 450 and 550 g when fully extended. Renew if unserviceable.

6 Reverse the foregoing operations to reassemble and refit. Very lightly grease the pivot 'a' and the fibre 'b' on the breaker arm. If the capacitor is suspect, the best test is by substitution.

3:4 Removing and refitting ignition cam and centrifugal advance mechanism. Setting centrifugal advance

Access to the cam and centrifugal weights mechanism is obtained by removing the ignition box housing as described in **Section 3:3**. Remove the protective cover, then referring to **FIGS 3:6** and **3:7**, remove the circlip 2, the thrust washer 3, the cam 4 and the two weights assemblies 5. Clean all the components. Lightly oil the pivots 'a' and the end of the camshaft, then refit the components in the reverse order of their dismantling, locating the advance weights as shown in the illustration. On completion check the points gap (see **Section 3:2**) and the timing (see **Section 3:5**).

Other than by using a stroboscopic light, an angle dephaser and a tachometer, which may not always be available, service agents use a special Fenwick testing apparatus No. 1692.T (see **FIG 3:8**) for checking the

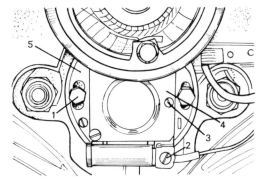

FIG 3:5   Ignition box removal from cam and weights

Key to Fig 3:5   1 Ignition box retaining bolts   2 Terminal screw   3 Cover screw   4 Cover   5 Backplate

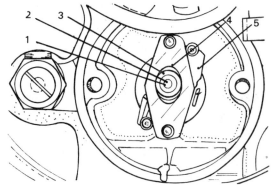

FIG 3:6   Cam and advance weights mechanism

Key to Fig 3:6   1 End of camshaft   2 Circlip   3 Thrust washer   4 Cam   5 Advance weights

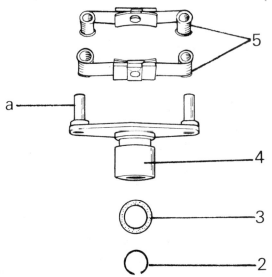

FIG 3:7   An exploded view of the cam and weights

Key to Fig 3:7   2 Circlip   3 Thrust washer   4 Cam   5 Advance weights   a Pivots

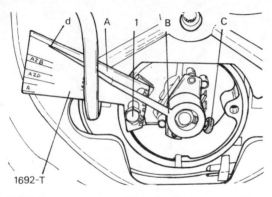

FIG 3:8 Apparatus used for checking the centrifugal advance

Key to Fig 3:   1 Ignition box retaining bolt
A Graduated plate   **B** Needle holder   **C** Retaining screw
d Indicating needle on the zero mark

centrifugal advance mechanism when required. The instrument is secured in place behind the bolt head 1 retaining the ignition box and the pointer carrier B located on the ignition cam and secured by the screw C. To use the instrument, turn the engine by the flywheel to bring the pointer to the zero mark at 'd'. Move the pointer carrier anticlockwise without forcing it until it reaches the end of its travel with no movement of the flywheel or camshaft. The pointer should then lie in the AZP sector, representing an advance of 10 to 15 deg. (engines A79/1, M28/1 and M/28), midway between the AZP and AZB sectors for an advance of 7.5 to 12.5 deg. (engines A79/0) or in sector AZB for engines A53 or M4. If the pointer falls outside the specified areas adjustment should be made by bending the stop on each weight, ensuring that the weights abut simultaneously on their individual stops.

3:5 Retiming ignition

To check or time the ignition, remove the fan as previously described and insert a rod of 6 mm diameter and of a convenient length into the hole provided on the lefthand side of the crankcase. Turn the engine by hand until the rod enters a similar hole provided in the flywheel, when the engine will be situated at the point of ignition for the specified timing advance. Proceed as follows:

1 Connect a test lamp between the ignition coil primary terminal, coloured blue, and a good earth on the chassis. Disconnect the sparking plugs to prevent the engine from starting and switch on the ignition.
2 Remove the ignition box cover and bring the advance weights together by hand to their initial position. Loosen the two bolts retaining the ignition box in place and turn the box whilst observing the exact moment when the points separate, when the test

lamp will light. Tighten the securing bolts and refit the cover.
3 Remove the rod inserted in the flywheel and turn the engine in its normal direction of rotation and stop when the lamp lights up again after one revolution. The test rod should now again enter the hole in the flywheel. If the hole has passed the rod the ignition is retarded and the timing on this cylinder must be adjusted. The advance must not be less than 12 deg. (engines A53, A79/0, A79/1 and M4) or 8 deg. (engines M28/1 and M28). There should also be no more than 3 deg. difference between the timing point on one cylinder and the timing point on the other, which corresponds to one tooth plus a tooth gap on the flywheel ring gear. If this is exceeded the cam should be renewed. Note that turning the ignition box clockwise retards the ignition and anticlockwise advances the ignition.

3:6 Sparking plugs

Several different types of sparking plugs are specified for the various cars covered in this manual, of which a representative list is given in **Technical Data**. The plugs should be removed every 3000 miles to check the condition of the plug and the gap between the electrodes.

Unless specifically mentioned, the standard sparking plug gap is between .6 and .7 mm (.024 to .028 inch). This should be set by bending the side or earthed electrode as necessary.

Plugs can be cleaned and tested under working pressure on a blasting machine used by most service agents. A deposit of brown to greyish tan colour is the normal condition of a plug used for a mixed period of high and low speed driving. Wet black deposits indicate oil fouling and dry fluffy black deposits are caused by too rich a mixture or misfiring. Badly eroded electrodes will be a sign of overheating.

3:7 Fault diagnosis

(a) Engine will not fire

1 Battery discharged
2 Contact breaker points dirty, pitted or out of adjustment
3 Faulty cable or loose connection in LT circuit
4 Faulty coil
5 Broken contact breaker spring
6 Contact points stuck open

(b) Engine misfires

1 Check 2, 3 and 5 in (a)
2 Weak contact spring
3 HT plug and coil leads defective
4 Loose sparking plug
5 Sparking plug insulation cracked
6 Sparking plug gap incorrect
7 Ignition timing too far advanced

CHAPTER 4

THE CLUTCH

4:1 Construction and operation

The clutch assembly is of the single dry plate type of 185 mm diameter, with the optional addition of a centrifugal clutch mechanism automatically actuated by the rotational speed of the flywheel. The hub of the clutch disc (see **FIGS 4:1** and **4:2**) is free to slide along the splines or serrations of the main drive gear shaft, the end of which forms a spigot which fits into the clutch pilot bearing in the centre of the crankshaft.

The operation of the clutch is through the friction linings of the disc being sandwiched between the machined face of the flywheel and a pressure plate mounted in the clutch assembly. Six compression springs (see **FIG 4:3**) are fitted between the cover and the pressure plate, giving the necessary pressure when the cover is firmly attached to the flywheel. Movement of the pressure plate is obtained through three hinged levers or release fingers whose operation frees the clutch disc from the flywheel and the pressure plate. The levers are operated through a clutch release bearing and arm controlled by a cable from the clutch pedal.

The centrifugal clutch has the same basic features with the exception of a modified clutch disc. The centrifugal engagement (see **FIGS 4:4** and **4:5**) is effected by lined weighted segments carried on a flanged ring attached to the flywheel and enclosed in a drum incorporated in the clutch assembly and running on a ballbearing on the main drive shaft. A longer main segment riveted to the ring carries a shorter segment to which the lining is attached. The lining shoes are mounted on leaf springs, so that as the flywheel revolves they moves outwards under centrifugal force and come into contact with the inner circumferential surface of the drum. Both the normal and centrifugal types of clutches are operated by the clutch pedal in the same way except that centrifugal engagement is independent of clutch pedal action and the disc in centrifugal clutches operates on the face of the drum instead of directly on the flywheel. The thrust or release bearing, operating the release levers, is of the carbon ring type requiring no lubrication in vehicles before 1968 and a ballbearing in later models.

In running conditions the centrifugal clutch gives clutch disengagement as soon as the engine speed falls below a certain limit and a progressive engagement when accelerating above this limit. The vehicle can be stopped without applying the clutch pedal or stalling the engine and can be started again in first or second gear by merely pressing the accelerator pedal. In slow traffic

FIG 4:1 An exploded view of the clutch

gearchanges are unnecessary and it is needed only to change the acceleration rate to give first or second gear running. These conditions apply up to about 1000 rev/min, when the clutch operates in the normal way and the pedal is used to declutch for changing gear.

4:2 Routine maintenance

Several factors may affect good clutch operation. Periodical inspection should be made of the condition of the operating linkage, including the pedal shaft and also of the engine mountings.

The clutch pedal height should be maintained as shown in FIG 4:6. With the clutch pedal released the height 'm' from the corner of the pedal pad to the floor should be 130 ± 5 mm on the 2CV4, 2CV6 and Dyane models, or between 117 and 120 mm on the Ami. If otherwise, adjust by bending the support shown at 'a'.

To adjust the pedal free travel, loosen the locknut 2 and turn the nut 1 to obtain a play of 1 to 1.5 mm between the release bearing and the fingers, which corresponds to a movement of 20 to 25 mm at the clutch pedal. Retighten the locknut, then run the engine and ensure that the gears engage correctly when declutching.

On AK vans (see FIG 4:7), place the vehicle on a lift or over a pit and remove the panel under the crankcase after unscrewing the six retaining bolts. Loosen the locknut 2 and adjust the nut 3 until the release bearing on withdrawal makes contact with the release fingers without pressure. Then unscrew the nut three or four turns to obtain a free travel at the end of the clutch fork. Tighten the locknut, check the adjustment and refit the panel.

At intervals a little engine oil should be applied to the operating cable. This can be done quite simply with an oil can.

4:3 Clutch removal and refitting

With the engine removed and separated from the gearbox as described in Chapter 1, remove the retaining screws of the clutch mechanism and withdraw the clutch disc and the pressure plate assembly. Further dismantling of the pressure plate assembly is not advised, as in coil

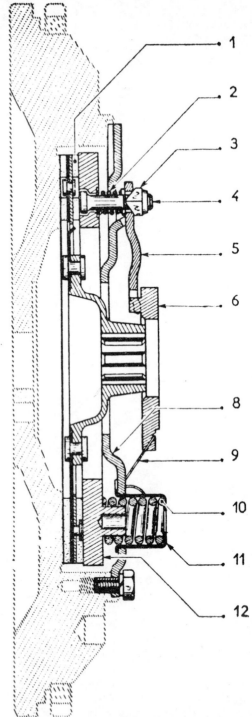

FIG 4:2 A sectional view of the clutch

Key to Fig 4:2   1 Clutch disc linings   2 Adjusting screw   3 Nut   4 Release lever adjusting screws   5 Release levers   6 Thrust plate   8 Cover   9 Locating springs   10 Compression springs   11 Cups   12 Pressure plate

spring clutches special jigs are necessary for both dismantling and reassembling and it follows that the work is more suitably undertaken by a service agent.

In the case of centrifugal clutches, remove the clutch drum as follows:

1 Remove the fork lever and engage first gear.

2 Remove the metal tapped over to lock the thread and unscrew the bearing retaining nut 4 (see **FIG 4:5**) which has a lefthand thread. Do not allow the spanner to bear sideways on the main drive shaft during this operation.

3 Remove the clutch drum 3 (see **FIG 4:3**) and the clutch assembly 2. Disengage the clutch mechanism 2, the disc and the adjusting spacer 5 (see **FIG 4:5**).

4 If required, the bearing 6 can be pressed out with the aid of a mandrel of 22 mm diameter and ·50 mm long after removing the bearing retaining ring 7 with two screwdrivers. Note that this ring must be renewed on refitting.

Examine the mating faces of the pressure plate and flywheel or drum for wear or scores. Procedure if refacing is necessary is described in **Chapter 1**. The inner circumferential surface of the drum on which the weighted

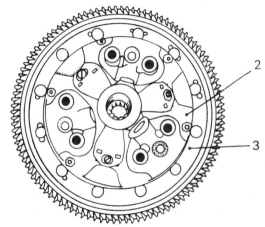

FIG 4:3   A view of the clutch mechanism showing: 2 the release levers, the spring cups and the retaining nuts and 3 the drum assembly

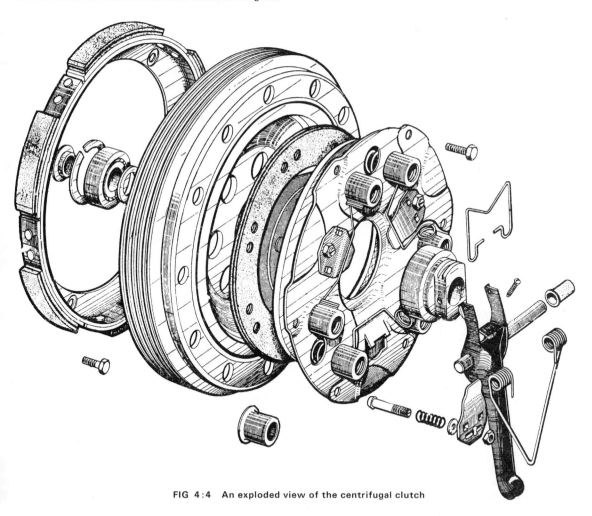

FIG 4:4   An exploded view of the centrifugal clutch

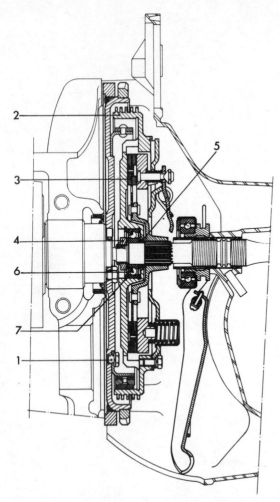

FIG 4:5   Sectional views of the centrifugal clutch

Key to Fig 4:5   1 Bolts attaching ring assembly to flywheel   2 Clutch drum   3 Disc   4 Bearing locknut 5 Adjusting spacer   6 Bearing   7 Bearing retaining ring

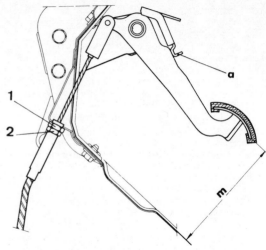

FIG 4:6   Adjusting clutch pedal free play

Key to Fig 4:6   1 Adjusting nut   2 Locknut   a Stop lever m Pedal clearance

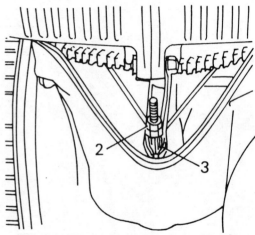

FIG 4:7   Clutch adjustment nuts on AK vans

linings bear is not rectifiable and if unserviceable the drum must be renewed. Similarly the weights and linings themselves are not separately serviced. Their balance and concentricity are carefully adjusted during manufacture and if wear or other defects occur the complete ring as an asssembly must be renewed. Inspect the clutch spigot bearing. If renewal is necessary it can be extracted by a slide hammer tool No. 1671.T. Examine the disc or driven plate as described in **Section 4:4**.

To remove and refit the release bearing, referring to **FIG 4:8**, proceed as follows:

1 Disengage the clip 1 by pulling back its ends, then withdraw the hub support 2 to remove the release bearing.

2 Lightly oil the hub support and engage the bearing on the hub. Align the clip securing holes in the bearing with those in the release fork.

3 Locate the central straight part of the clip 1 in the groove of the bearing and fit the ends of the clip into the securing holes. Ensure that the bearing is correctly locked in place.

Removal of the clutch fork if required is obtained by removing the shaft retaining bolt 5 and pulling the shaft as far as it will go to the right, through the aperture in the clutch housing. The lefthand side spring coils and anti-rattle bush 7 can then be removed, followed by those on the opposite side and the fork withdrawn. Refit in the reverse order of the dismantling operations.

To refit the clutch, ensure that the disc slides freely on the main drive shaft splines or serrations and that all mating surfaces are perfectly clean (see **Section 4:4**). Refit the clutch to the flywheel, using either a spare main drive shaft or a special locating tool as described in **Chapter 1**.

In centrifugal clutches refit the bearing in the clutch

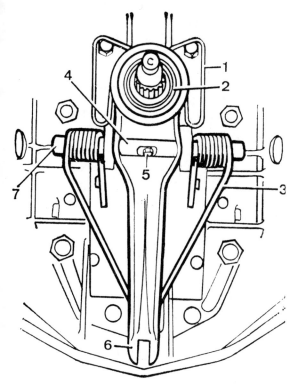

FIG 4:8   Details of the clutch fork assembly

Key to Fig 4:8   1 Clip   2 Hub support   3 Spring   4 Shaft
5 Fork shaft retaining bolt   6 Fork   7 Anti-rattle bush

drum if removed and the same adjusting spacer as originally fitted, greasing the collar. Locate the disc, centring it as in normal clutches, and fit the pressure plate assembly, tightening the bolts and spring washers. Lock the drive shaft by engaging a gear and fit the drum. Tighten the retaining nut with lefthand thread to a torque of 3 to 4 kg m, again taking care as in removal not to bear upon the drive shaft. Peen the metal to lock the nut. Fully support the nut so that the oil throwback blades do not impinge on the housing bore. Finally, refit the clutch fork lever.

If the drive shaft or gearbox housing has been renewed it will be necessary for the position of the clutch drum to be adjusted to ensure the correct location of the centrifugal weights. The adjustment is made by selecting a bearing spacer (5 in FIG 4:5) of the correct thickness and with the aid of a special straightedge fitted with a dial indicator as shown in FIG 4:9. Procedure is as follows:

1 Set the dial indicator at zero with the straightedge on a surface plate.
2 Place an adjusting spacer 3.1 mm thick on the drive shaft and position the drum on the shaft without the clutch disc or mechanism. Temporarily tighten the nut.
3 Measure with the dial indicator the distance 'a' between the face of the gearbox housing and the face of the drum which receives the bearing.
4 If this dimension is, say, 5.65 mm, it should be between 5.12 and 5.14 mm for the drum to be correctly

positioned. The drum would therefore have to be moved forward by 5.65 mm less 5.42 mm, i.e. .23 mm and an adjusting spacer selected .23 mm thicker than the one measured. It follows that a 3.3 mm adjusting spacer is required.

5 Adjusting spacers available are in the range of 2.5 to 4 mm with increments of .3 mm, hence the spacer chosen would be one of 3.4 mm.

The remaining refitting operations are then as already described. When locating the drum on the drive shaft it will help to use a finger to guide the adjusting spacer to ease the entry of the shaft.

4:4 Driven plate condition

The driven plate or clutch disc, also the centrifugal weighted linings, should be examined for excessive wear and signs of overheating. Check that the friction linings are secure and free from oil. A polished glaze on the linings is normal, but they should be light in colour with the grain clearly visible. A much darker colour obliterating the grain is a sign of oil on the linings, which can cause clutch slip or possibly difficulty in disengagement. If this condition is found, or the linings worn down to the rivet heads, it is advised that the complete disc assembly should be renewed in preference to riveting new linings on the existing assembly. As previously stated, if the centrifugal linings need renewal a new complete ring assembly will need to be fitted.

It should be ensured that the hub splines or serrations are not excessively worn. A good sliding fit with no slackness should be evident when they are engaged with the gearbox first motion shaft.

4:5 Renewing the clutch cable

To renew a clutch cable, refer to FIGS 4:10 and 4:11 and unscrew the locknut 4 and the adjusting nut 3. Withdraw the end of the cable 2 from the pedal clevis 1 and then raise the car on firm supports (see Hints on Maintenance in the Appendix).

Detach the end of the cable 6 from the clutch fork and disengage the cable and sheath assembly.

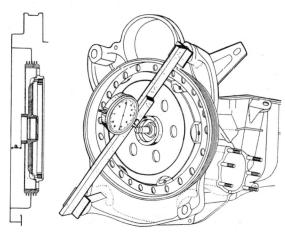

FIG 4:9   Clutch drum adjustment with straightedge and dial gauge, showing measurement to be made at a

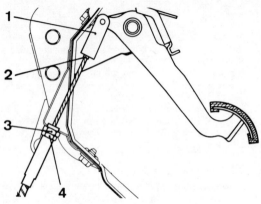

FIG 4:10 Clutch cable connection

Key to Fig 4:10 1 Clevis 2 Cable end 3 Adjusting nut 4 Locknut

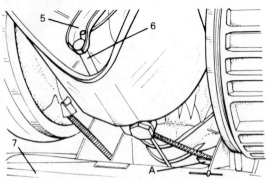

FIG 4:11 Clutch cable connection

Key to Fig 4:11 5 Connection to clutch fork 6 Cable end 7 Exhaust A Retaining clip

To fit a new cable, offer it from the rear of the gearbox. Guide the cable between the retainer A and the gearbox so that the cable avoids contact with the exhaust system 7. Lightly grease the end of the cable 6 and attach it to the clutch fork 5. Insert the other end of the cable through the floor and attach it to the pedal clevis 1. Lower the vehicle to the ground and adjust the pedal free travel as described in **Section 4:2**.

4:6 Fault diagnosis

(a) Clutch drag or spin

1 Excessive play in clutch cable
2 Oil or grease on linings
3 Flywheel face not running true
4 Misalignment between engine and gearbox
5 Clutch disc binding on splines or serrations
6 Main drive pinion (first motion shaft) binding in spigot bearing
7 Clutch disc distorted
8 Pressure plate distorted
9 Disc linings broken
10 Dirt or foreign matter in clutch

(b) Clutch fierce or judders

1 Check 2, 3, 4 and 7 in (a)
2 Worn clutch linings
3 Pressure plate not parallel with flywheel face
4 Contact area of linings not evenly distributed
5 Bent main drive pinion (first motion shaft)
6 Faulty engine or gearbox mountings
7 Backlash in transmission

(c) Clutch slip

1 Check 2, 3 and 4 in (a)

(d) Rattles and knocks

1 Badly worn splines in disc hub
2 Release bearing loose on fork
3 Play in main drive spigot bearing
4 Loose flywheel

CHAPTER 5

THE TRANSMISSION AND DRIVE SHAFTS

5:1 General description

The front wheel drive system is one in which the engine, gearbox, differential and final drive shafts are assembled as a compact unit. Power generated by the engine is transmitted to the gearbox through the flywheel and clutch on the end of the crankshaft. From the clutch the drive is taken up by the upper of the two parallel shafts in the gearbox shown in FIG 5:1 which carry the gearwheels providing changes of engine speed and power according to driving requirements. A final drive pinion is located on the end of the lower shaft, continuing the drive through the crownwheel and differential assembly to the drive shafts and the front wheels.

The gearbox has four forward ratios and one reverse, with synchromesh engagement of the forward gears. The engagement of the gears in the various ratios is shown in FIG 5:2 and the relative positions of the gearlever mounted on the scuttle in FIG 5:3. Three selector forks are installed for the engagement of first and reverse gears, second and third gears and also the fourth gear. The differential gear transmits the drive on each side through single or double universal ball joints, according to model, to the front road wheels.

5:2 Maintenance

The gearbox oil level should be checked every 5000 km and topped up if necessary to the bottom of the filler plug shown in FIG 5:4. A 21 mm ring spanner is normally used to remove the plug. Lubrication is thus provided for the combined gearbox/differential assembly and the specified oil is SAE.EP 80. The oil should be changed every 20,000 km, first removing the plug in the bottom of the gearbox to drain the assembly. After refitting the plug fill the gearbox to the required level with the specified oil. The capacity of the assembly is approximately .9 litre.

An approved grease should be applied every 5000 km to the nipples provided on the splined connections of the drive shafts (see FIG 5:21).

5:3 Gearbox removal and construction

The gearbox should be drained and detached from the engine after the removal of the engine/gearbox assembly as described in Chapter 1. A general view of the gearbox is shown in FIG 5:5 and access to the gears, of which the main components are shown in FIGS 5:6, 5:7 and

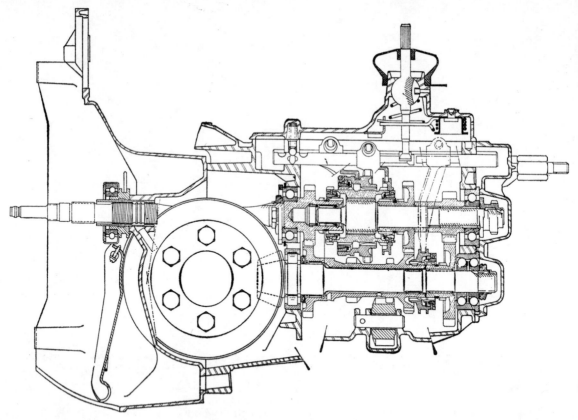

FIG 5:1 A sectional view of the gearbox

5:8, is obtained by removing the top and rear covers. Servicing operations on the mechanism are necessarily limited by the facilities available for precise reassembly after dismantling and which are only ordinarily to be found in a well-equipped service workshop. Dismantling operations present no serious difficulties but reassembly needs observance of very precise limits for clearances and fits in both differential gear (see **FIG 5:9**) and final drive. In particular the precise adjustment of the final drive pinion needs special care and experience, because an incorrect setting of the gear teeth will result in noisy operation and reducing the life of the gear. Special tools and workshop equipment as well as practical experience are required and it follows that the complete stripping and reassembly of a gearbox should be undertaken only be a qualified service agent. Alternatively a replacement unit on an exchange basis is advised, as an overhaul usually requires the renewal of all the parts.

5:4 Gearchange dismantling and reassembly

Details of the gearlever and its connections to the selector shafts and shift forks are shown in **FIG 5:10**. Dismantling of the fork assembly is undertaken by removing the screws securing the forks to the shafts and then removing the latter with a slight turning movement.

The selector forks are withdrawn for the first and reverse gear, also the second and third gear, but the fourth gear fork requires the removal of the mainshaft for its withdrawal. Note that when removing the shafts a finger should be placed over the holes for the shaft detent balls (see **FIG 5:11**) to prevent the ejection of the balls under the tension of the locking springs. If required, the balls and springs may later be removed by a magnetized rod and a wire hook.

Reassembly and adjustment are carried out as follows:
1 Fit the second/third and the first/reverse shift forks in their sliding gear grooves with the retaining screws facing to the left.
2 Locate the locking ball springs 10 and 6 for the fourth and first/reverse selector shafts. Lubricate the three shafts.
3 Engage the fourth gear selector shaft on the housing, with the locking slots at the front, and then in the fork but without engaging it in the front of the housing. Locate the balls 7 and 9 smeared with grease.
4 Fit the second/third selector shaft 8, the locking slots to the front, and then in its fork. Insert the ball 3 smeared with grease and locate the shaft in the neutral position.
5 Fit the first/reverse selector shaft 4, slots at the front, and then in its fork. Grease the ball 5 and locate it on

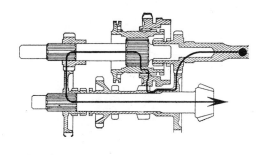

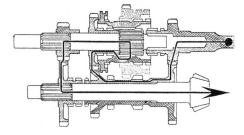

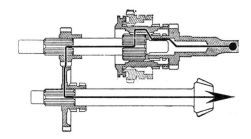

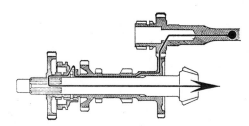

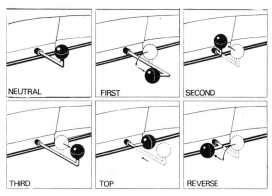

FIG 5:3   Gearlever positions

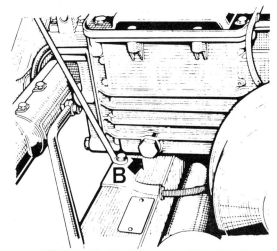

FIG 5:4   Position of gearbox filling plug

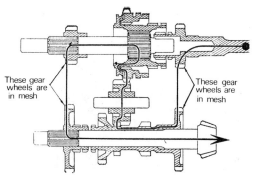

These gear wheels are in mesh

These gear wheels are in mesh

FIG 5:2   Diagrams showing engagement of gears. Top to bottom: First, Second, Third, Fourth, Reverse

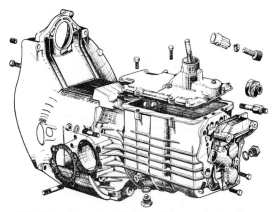

FIG 5:5   An exploded view of the gearbox casing

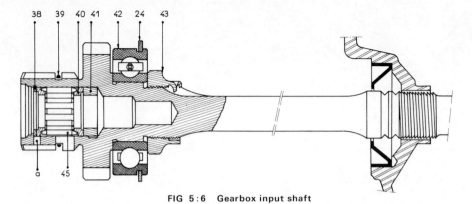

FIG 5:6 Gearbox input shaft

Key to Fig 5:6 24 Circlip 38 Needle bearing retainer 39 Synchronizing ring 40 Bearing retaining rings 41 Spacer 42 Bearing 43 Nut 45 Needle bearing

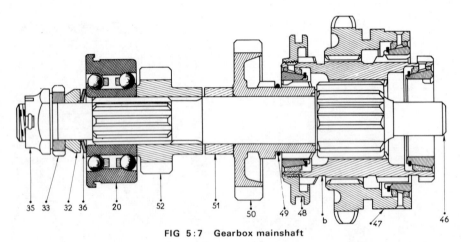

FIG 5:7 Gearbox mainshaft

Key to Fig 5:7 20 Bearing 32 Spacer 33 Speedometer nut 35 Castellated nut 36 Flexible ring 46 Shaft 47 First and reverse sliding gear 48 Second and third sliding gear 49 Synchronizing ring 50 Second gear 51 Spacer 52 Reduction pinion

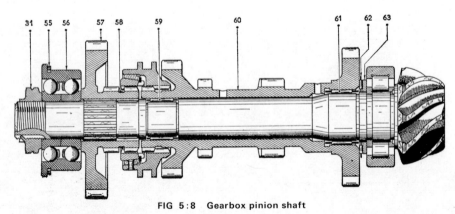

FIG 5:8 Gearbox pinion shaft

Key to Fig 5:8 31 Nut 55 Shims 56 Bearing 57 Reduction gear 58 Synchronizer ring 59 Needle bearing 60 Intermediate gear train 61 Needle bearing 62 Bearing retainer 63 Washer

the spring 6, then compress the ball and spring assembly with the aid of a suitable rod and complete the engagement of the shaft in its front location.

6 Fit the ball 11 and spring 10 similarly to complete the engagement of the fourth gear selector shaft. Locate the fourth and first/reverse selector shafts in neutral, refit the rear cover and fit the locking balls retaining plug.

Adjustment of the forks is undertaken as follows:

1 To adjust the second/third shift fork, ensure that the selector shaft is in the neutral position. To assist in holding the spring a collar No. MR.630.64/21 is available. Locate the special adjusting spacer No. 1786.T (see **FIG 5:12**) of thickness 1.8 mm on the mainshaft synchronizing ring as shown in **FIG 5:13**. Unscrew the fork nut and bring the second/third sliding gear 2 (see **FIG 5:14**) into contact with the adjusting tool. Then tighten the fork nut and withdraw the tool.

2 To adjust the first/reverse shift fork, ensure that the second/third and first/reverse selector shafts are positioned in neutral. Loosen the fork nut and locate the first/reverse sliding gear 1 (see **FIG 5:13**) to the middle of its engagement with the second/third sliding gear. This will align the rear face 'a' (see **FIG 5:14**) of the first/reverse gear with the rear machined end of the second/third gear. Tighten the two fork nuts.

3 To adjust the fourth gear shift fork, an adjusting spacer No. 3153.T (2.7 mm) is used, except on Dyane vehicles before March, 1968, which require a spacer 1785.T (1.55 mm). Ensure that the fourth gear selector shaft is in neutral then locate the spacer on the synchronizing ring of the reduction gear as shown in **FIG 5:15**. Loosen the fork screw then bring the fourth gear 3 into contact with the spacer tool. Tighten the fork nut and remove the spacer. Check the engagement of all gears and refit the gearbox cover.

Removal and refitting of the gearchange control lever shown in **FIG 5:16** is undertaken by first removing the retaining pin and disconnecting the lever 1. Then disconnect the earth wires 2 and remove the lever and the support 3 as an assembly. Refit by reversing the removal procedure, refilling the support cavity with grease as may be necessary.

5:5 Refitting the gearbox

Before locating the gearbox on the engine check that the bores of the two centring dowels on the crankcase are not worn oval or otherwise deformed. If unserviceable an incorrect alignment of engine and gearbox will follow, resulting in early deterioration of the clutch disc and mechanism. If wear in the bores is found excessive it will be necessary to renew either the crankcase or the gearbox housing or both. Following this preliminary inspection, engage a gear and locate the gearbox on the engine, inserting the end of the first motion shaft in the pilot bearing. A smooth engagement of the gearbox with the engine should result, with rotating the assembly slightly as necessary to engage the splines on the shaft with the flutes in the hub of the clutch disc. Ensure that the clutch housing and engine casing are in contact then tighten the gearbox securing bolts and serrated washers.

FIG 5:9　An exploded view of the differential gear

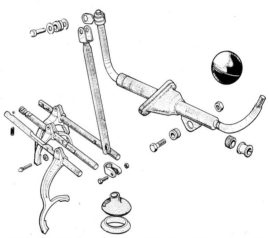

FIG 5:10　An exploded view of the gearchange assembly

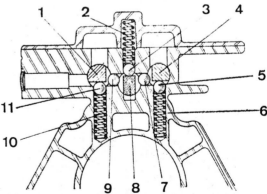

FIG 5:11　Arrangement of fork shafts and locking balls

Key to Fig 5:11　　1 Fourth gear selector shaft　　2 Spring
3 Ball　4 First/reverse gear selector shaft　5 Ball　6 Spring
7 Ball　8 Second/third gear selector shaft　9 Ball　10 Spring
11 Ball

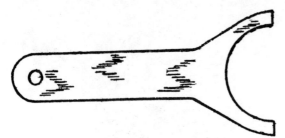

FIG 5:12 Fork adjusting tool No. 1786.T

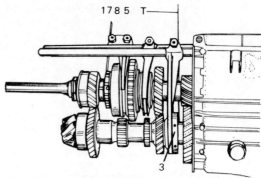

FIG 5:15 Adjusting the fourth gear selector fork, showing the fourth gear at 3

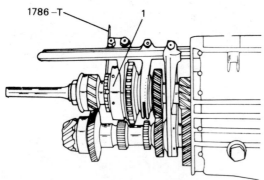

FIG 5:13 Adjusting the second and third gear selector fork, showing the first and reverse gear at 1

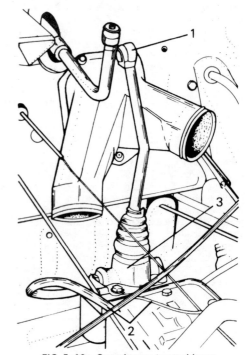

FIG 5:16 Gearchange control lever

Key to Fig 5:16 1 Intermediate shaft 2 Earth connections 3 Gearlever support

5:6 Removing and refitting the drive shafts

Power is transmitted to the front wheels from the differential gear by drive shafts (see **FIGS 5:17** and **5:18**) on each side of the front brake assemblies. As these shafts can revolve at considerable angles, special universal ball joints of the single or double constant velocity type, according to model, are incorporated in their assembly. Operations to remove and refit a drive shaft on the wheel side are as follows:

1 Raise the front of the vehicle and fit firm supports under the front axle. Remove the wheel.
2 Referring to **FIG 5:19**, remove the splitpin 2 and the hub nut 1, holding the hub by inserting a drift or other

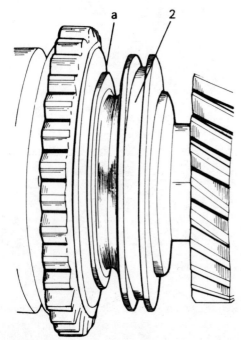

FIG 5:14 The rear face a of the first and reverse gear and the second and third sliding gear 2

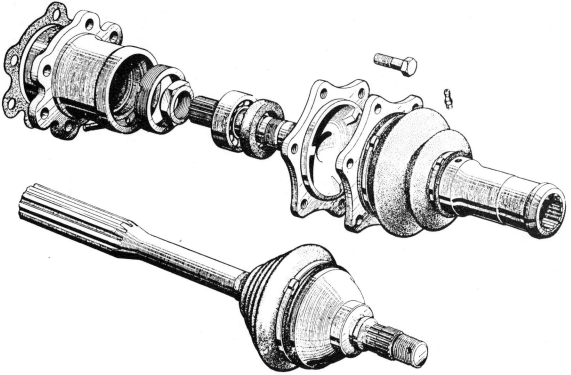

FIG 5:17   An exploded view of the drive shafts with single universal ball joints

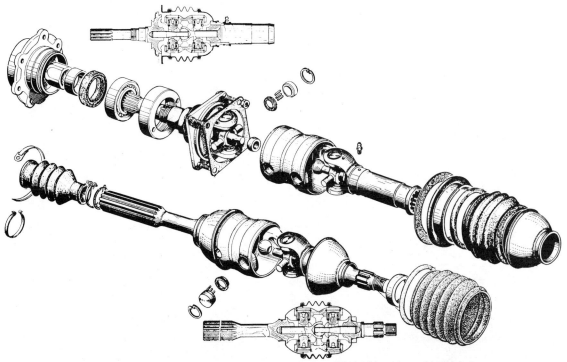

FIG 5:18   An exploded view of the drive shafts with double universal ball joints

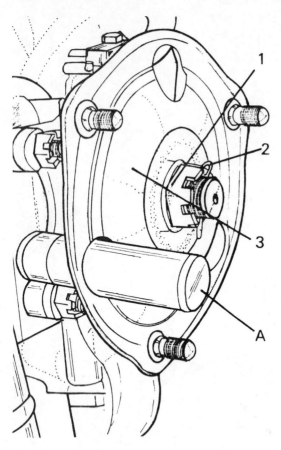

FIG 5:19 Removing the front hub nut 1, showing the retaining pin 2, the hub 3 and the holding tool **A**

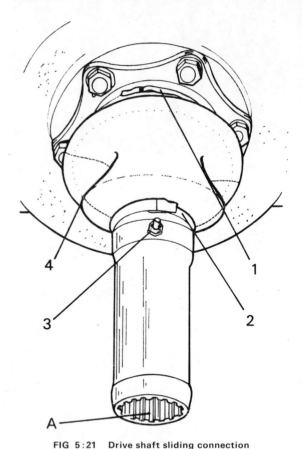

FIG 5:21   Drive shaft sliding connection

Key to Fig 5:21   1/2 Clips   3 Lubricating nipple   4 Boot
A Internal serrations

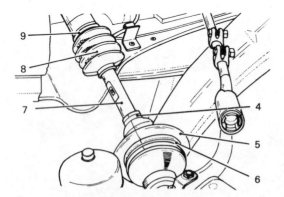

FIG 5:20   Removing a drive shaft on the wheel side

Key to Fig 5:20   4 Clip   5 Boot   6 Clip   7 Shaft
8 Boot   9 Clip

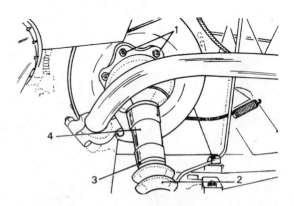

FIG 5:22   Removing a drive shaft on the gearbox side

Key to Fig 5:22   1 Flange retaining nuts   2 Boot   3 Clip
4 Shaft

tool into one of the holes as shown. Rest the tool against the stub axle carrier and not under the steering lever which might be damaged. Also support the axle carrier on a chock to prevent damage to the radius arm stop.

3 Turn the steering to full lock, loosen the boot clip 9 (see **FIG 5:20**) and disengage the boot 8. Withdraw the shaft 7.

4 Carefully inspect the boot 5 to ensure that it is in good condition, as any leakage will soon damage the constant velocity joint. If doubtful, renew it and ensure that the securing clamps 4 and 6 are correctly tightened. Do not clean the joint by immersing it in any fluid.

5 To refit, check that the boot on the transmission side is properly positioned and serviceable. Grease the splines and serrations (A in **FIG 5:21**) and push the shaft fully home, then attach the hub nut, tighten it to a torque of 35 to 40 kgm and insert a new splitpin.

Fit the boot 8 (see **FIG 5:20**) and its clip 9 then lower the vehicle to the ground.

The same preliminary operations are undertaken for the drive shaft on the gearbox side. First loosen the clip 3 (see **FIG 5:22**) and disengage the boot 2. After removing the six bolts 1 retaining the shaft, the splines can then be withdrawn and the shaft disengaged. When refitting the shaft grease the splines and secure the six

attaching bolts to a torque of 5 to 6 kgm. New bolts should always be fitted. Ensure that the boot is fully serviceable and secure it by the clip. Refit the wheel and tighten the nuts to 5 to 6 kgm.

5:7 Fault diagnosis

(a) Jumping out of gear

1 Excessively worn locating slots in striking fork rods
2 Selector fork locking screws loose
3 Worn synchromesh units

(b) Noisy gearbox

1 Insufficient oil
2 Worn or damaged bearings
3 Worn or damaged gear teeth

(c) Difficulty in engaging gear

1 Incorrect clutch pedal adjustment
2 Worn synchromesh cones

(d) Oil leaks

1 Worn or damaged oil seals
2 Covers loose or faces damaged, defective joints

NOTES

CHAPTER 6

FRONT AXLE ASSEMBLY AND HUBS

6:1 General description

The general arrangement of the front axle assembly on Ami vehicles is shown in **FIG 6 : 1**. Tubular arms attached to the stub axles on each side are incorporated with the steering rack housing and secured to a crossmember. The axle and steering rack assembly may thus be removed as a unit after disconnecting the crossmember from the chassis and releasing the boots of the drive shafts on the wheel sides to enable the shafts to slide out of their mountings. Friction dampers are fitted on the studs of the crossmember where the arms are attached.

The front hub bearings are of the double row ball type packed with grease retained by sealing rings on both sides. The hub and bearings (see **FIG 6 : 2**) form a unit with the steering knuckle assembly, which includes the swivel pin housing and tubular arm attachments at the bottom and the steering lever connection at the top. Grease nipples are provided at the base of each steering pivot, into which an approved lubricant should be injected every 5000 km.

6:2 Front hub bearings renewal

If excessive slackness or roughness develops in the front hub bearings it is necessary to remove the hub for examination and overhaul operations as follows.

1 Lift and firmly support the vehicle with a block of wood under the axle crossmember, as shown in **FIG 6 : 3**. Remove the wheel, then remove the outer drive shaft as described in **Chapter 5**.

2 Support the axle arm, then drive out the hub from the pivot with the aid of a suitable drift (see **FIG 6 : 4**).

3 Drill out the punch marks which lock the ring nut 4 (see **FIG 6 : 2**) with a 4 mm drill, then remove the ring nut with the special tool 3301.T (see **FIG 6 : 5**) without its guide but with the fitting 3303.T for nuts with two notches or 3302.T for nuts with four notches.

4 Drive out the bearing from its bore with a bronze drift. The inner race of the bearing will probably remain on the hub and can be removed with an extractor 1813.T. Remove the oil seals from the housing and the ring nut. Carefully clean all parts.

5 Reassemble by fitting the sealing ring 12 (see **FIG 6 : 2**) in the ring nut, the lips of the seal to face towards the bearing. The sealing ring must be located so that it is 1.25 to 1.30 mm from the bearing thrust collar.

6 Fit the sealing ring 3 in the hub bore, with a clearance of .1 to .5 mm from the bearing thrust collar.

7 Check the condition of the bearings by attaching the two inner cages with a bolt and two washers and

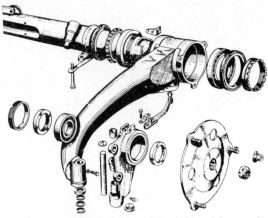

FIG 6:1 An exploded view of the lefthand front axle arm, steering housing and hub components

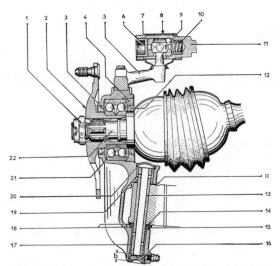

FIG 6:2 A sectional view of a front hub and steering pivot assembly

Key to Fig 6:2 1 Nut 2 Hub 3 Sealing ring 4 Ring nut 5 Steering lever 6 End nut 7 Ball seat 8 Casing 9 Ball seat 10 Spring 11 Track rod 12 Sealing ring 13 Swivel pin housing 14 Dust cover 15 Friction washer 16 End plug 17 Lower sleeve 18 Thrust washers 19 Upper sleeve 20 Expanding plug 21 Bearing 22 Shaft

examining for play. Then grease the bearing and fit it in the bore of the hub with the aid of a tube of external diameter 70 mm applied to the outer cage.

8 Attach and tighten the ring nut to a torque of 35 to 40 kgm, employing the tools used for its removal. Lock the ring by peening it in two places. Refit the hub by tapping it home with a mallet. Finally reassemble the items removed for access in Operation 1.

6:3 Removing and refitting swivel pin

To remove a swivel pin it is necessary first to remove the outer drive shaft (see **Chapter 5**) and the inertia

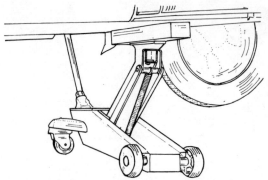

FIG 6:3 Supporting the chassis under the crossmember when raising the vehicle

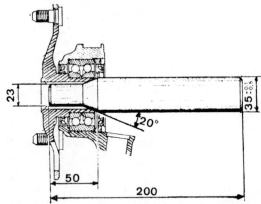

FIG 6:4 Dimensions (in mm) of a tool for removing the hub

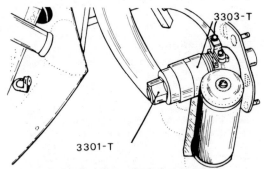

FIG 6:5 Removing the hub ring nut

damper. Further operations are as follows:

1 Detach the steering lever, using a tool such as that shown in **FIG 6:6**.

2 Loosen the attachment of the end plug 16 (see **FIG 6:2**) and remove it with a screwdriver.

3 Remove the expanding plug 20 using an 8 mm diameter drift and then the swivel pin with the aid of a special tool No. 3742 or 1858.T as shown in **FIG 6:7**. It is possible that a workshop press may have to be employed, which will necessitate the removal of the axle arm.

4 Proceed to remove the cap 1 (see **FIG 6:8**), the

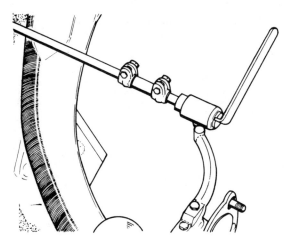

FIG 6:6   Disconnecting the steering lever

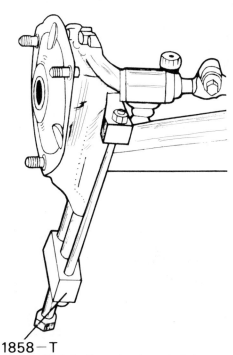

1858−T

FIG 6:7   Removing the swivel pin

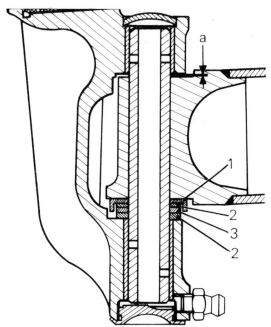

FIG 6:8   A sectional view of the swivel pin housing

Key to Fig 6:8   1 Retaining cap   2 Thrust washers
3 Friction washer   a .1 to .4 mm

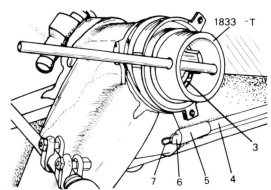

FIG 6:9   Removing the axle arm retaining nut

Key to Fig 6:9   3 Slotted nut   4 Suspension tie rod
5 Screwed link   6 V-pivot   7 Securing pin

thrust washers 2 and the friction washer 3. If required, remove and overhaul the hub as described in the previous Section.

Refitting is undertaken as follows:

1 Prepare a dummy swivel pin with a tapered end, 16.5 mm diameter and 150 mm long. Locate the thrust and friction washers in the cap 1. Introduce the pin and engage the washer assembly from the bottom, using the dummy pin to position the items correctly.

2 Measure the clearance at the point 'a' in **FIG 6:8**, which should be between .1 and .4 mm. Adjustment may be made by thrust washers of appropriate thick-

nesses.

3 Lubricate the upper and lower bushes 19 and 17 in **FIG 6:2**, then clean and lubricate the swivel pin and start its installation with a copper mallet. Position the lubrication holes as shown in the illustrations and complete the installation by using the special tool previously described or a press. The bottom of the swivel pin should be a distance 'b' (see **FIG 6:2**) of 7.10 to 7.25 mm from the base of the housing.

4 Pack the interior of the housing and the spaces under the upper and lower plugs with an approved grease. Tighten the lower plug with a screwdriver and peen

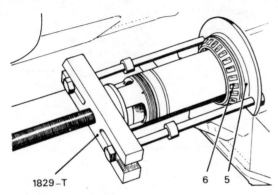

FIG 6:10 Removing an axle inner bearing 6 and joint 5

over the collar. Fit the expanding plug 20 and flatten it with a hammer, finally securing it by peening it into the carrier metal in four places.

5 Refit the items removed for access and further grease the swivel pin under pressure.

6:4 Removing and refitting the axle assembly

Operations to remove and refit an axle assembly on Ami vehicles are as follows:

1 Raise and firmly support the vehicle as shown in **FIG 6:3**. Remove the front wheels and loosen the handbrake adjusting nuts to their fullest extent. Remove the floor mat and front seat, take out the rubber plugs and loosen the gearbox retaining nuts by several turns. Disconnect the exhaust pipe.

2 Lift the gearbox with a jack with wooden blocks interposed to disengage the mounting studs.

3 Locate a wooden block approximately 35 mm thick between the gearbox and the chassis crossmember.

4 Remove the steering column on the Ami 8 or the steering tube on the Ami 6 (see **Chapter 9**). On Ami 8 vehicles, disconnect the anti-roll bar on the right-hand side, marking the position of its adjustment for later refitting. Remove the shock absorber brackets.

5 Make a paint mark on the screwed end of the suspension tie rod and its attachment, then remove the clips to disengage the arm. Refitting to the marks made will avoid alteration to the underbody heights or weight distribution. It is advised, however, that on completion of refitting operations the underbody heights should be checked as described in **Chapter 8**.

6 Disengage the steering lever and remove the splitpin and nut securing each drive shaft to the hub.

7 Withdraw the splitpin and remove the retaining nut to disengage the lefthand arm from the crossmember, using the special spanner No. 1833.T as shown in **FIG 6:9**. If necessary use a mallet to tap the arm at the rear

8 Proceed to remove the steering pinion (see **Chapter 9**), first placing a wooden batten approximately 8 mm thick in the crossmember to hold the steering rack during the operation. Remove the peened metal of the nut with a 4 mm drill after removing the sealing rings then remove the nut and take out the pinion for which a special tool No. 3503.T is available. Plug the pinion bore with one of the gearbox nut plugs.

9 Remove the securing bolts and withdraw the crossmember and righthand arm assembly as a complete unit.

10 The inner bearing 6 (see **FIG 6:10**) and its rubber joint 5 can be removed if required from the crossmember with the special puller tool No. 1829.T. Refitting is undertaken with the aid of tubes as in **FIG 6:11** showing the assembly of the outer bearing. Note that an SKF roller bearing must never be fitted in a Timken outer cage or the contrary, because the roller tapers differ. Two bearings of different makes, however, can be assembled on the same arm.

Other refitting operations are in general the reverse of those undertaken in dismantling. Particular features to be observed are as follows:

1 Check that the dowel pins of the crossmember are correctly located when refitting the assembly. Lubricate and refit the drive shafts as described in **Chapter 5**.

2 Lubricate the outer and inner bearings of the arms with an approved grease when attaching them to the crossmember and tighten the slotted nut to a torque of 6 kg m with the spanner No. 1833.T to position the bearings. Then slacken the nut and retighten it to a torque of 5 kg m. Fit a new splitpin, spread the ends and ensure that the arms turn freely.

3 Refit the anti-roll bar with the bend towards the rear of the vehicle and with the adjusting shims as re-

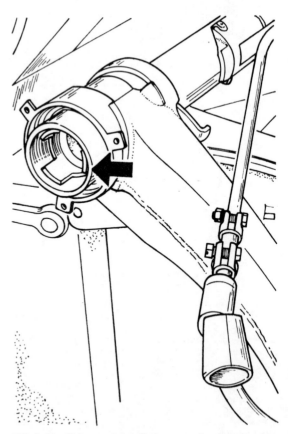

FIG 6:11 Tube used for fitting an axle outer bearing

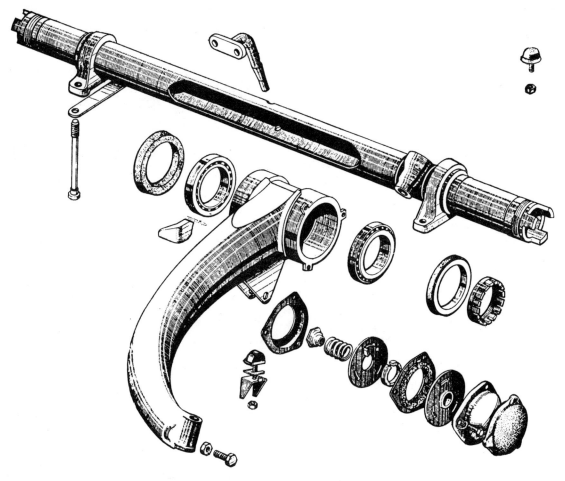

FIG 6:12   An exploded view of a front axle arm with friction damper

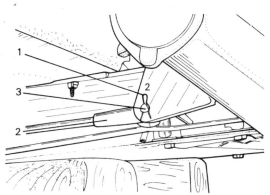

FIG 6:13   Suspension arm attachment, showing the securing pin 1, the screwed link 2 and the V-pivot 3

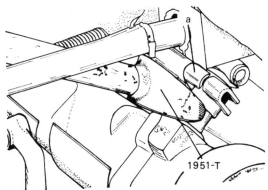

FIG 6:14   Disconnecting the steering pinion, showing collar 'a'

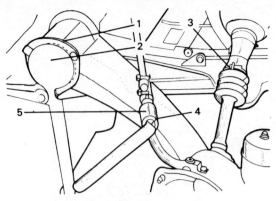

FIG 6:15   Disconnecting a track rod

Key to Fig 6:15   1 Clip   2 Damper outer cover   3 Boot clip   4 Splitpin   5 Sleeve

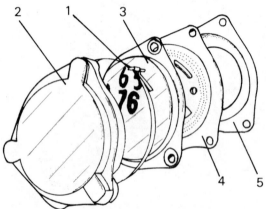

FIG 6:16   An exploded view of a friction damper

Key to Fig 6:16   1 Clip   2 Rubber outer cover
3 Protecting cover   4 Friction element   5 Seal

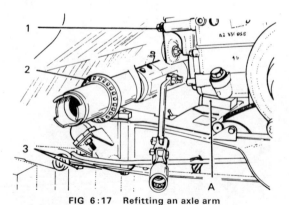

FIG 6:17   Refitting an axle arm

Key to Fig 6:17   1 Bolts securing gearbox to support on axle arm   2 Inner bearing   3 Bolts securing crossmember to chassis   A Wood supporting block

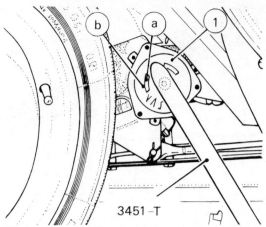

FIG 6:18   Assembling the friction damper 1 with the tool No. 3451.T to bring the apertures **b** opposite the studs **a**

moved. A clearance of 6 mm should be obtained between the bar and the arms. Tighten the securing bolts to a torque of 6 kg m.

4 Observe the marks made when refitting the suspension tie rods and lubricate the ball joints when refitting the track rods.

5 Lubricate the steering pinion and bearing with an approved grease and assemble with the aid of the wooden batten to hold the steering rack. Tighten the nut to a torque of 14 kg m and peen over the nut to secure it firmly.

Similar operations on Dyane and 2CV vehicles (see **FIG 6:12**) are as follows:

1 After raising the vehicle and obtaining access by removing the wings and side panels, remove the silencer connecting pipe on the righthand side.

2 Referring to **FIG 6:13**, disconnect the suspension tie rod without unscrewing the link 2. Remove one of the clips 1 and disengage the V-pivot 3. Remove the shock absorber brackets (if fitted).

3 Referring to **FIG 6:14**, remove the securing collar 'a' of the steering pinion, using if necessary the lever No. 1951.T to disengage the pinion. Refer to **Chapter 9** if a steering wheel lock is fitted.

4 Take out the splitpin 4 and then the nut with the spanner (see **FIG 6:15**) to detach the righthand track rod. If friction dampers are fitted, remove the clip 1, the rubber outer cover 2 and the protecting cover 3 (see **FIG 6:16**) to disengage the friction element 4 and the seal 5 from the studs of the crossmember.

5 Continue as in the previous operation 7 to remove the slotted nut and then to disengage the righthand axle arm and drive shaft from the crossmember.

6 Referring to **FIG 6:17**, remove the bolts 1 securing the gearbox to the rear flexible support, remove the two handbrake cable retaining screws and place a 35 mm thick block of wood between the gearbox and the chassis as shown at A. Remove the four bolts retaining the crossmember on the chassis, then disengage the lefthand arm and steering assembly from the lefthand side of the vehicle.

7 Reassembly comprises the reverse of the dismantling procedure, lubricating the various components as previously described. The lefthand arm is first refitted and then the righthand arm assembly.

8 When reassembling the friction damper element on the studs 'a' (see **FIG 6:18**) of the crossmember, bring the apertures 'b' opposite to the studs 'a' with the tool No. 3451.T and secure the element in place. Use the other end of the tool to bring the two lower holes into alignment.

6:5 Suspension geometry

Suspension geometry includes the castor, camber and steering pivot inclination angles. The castor angle is obtained by inclining the steering pivot and gives a self-centring action to the steering effort. Camber is an outward inclination of the tops of the front wheels to facilitate cornering. Steering pivot inclination indicates that the swivel pins or kingpins are inclined in opposite directions, so that their centre lines, if projected downwards, would meet the ground near the points of contact of the tyres.

The inclination angles are given in **Technical Data** in the **Appendix**. For checking the angles specially designed tools and gauges are required for precise measurement and it will be necessary to obtain the assistance of a service agent with the appropriate equipment. The castor angle is set during manufacture and is not adjustable.

6:6 Fault diagnosis

(a) Wheel wobble

1 Worn hub bearings
2 Uneven tyre wear
3 Loose wheel fixings
4 Uneven suspension springs

(b) 'Bottoming' of suspension

1 Dampers not working
2 Weak springs

(c) Heavy steering

1 Front tyres under-inflated
2 Ball joints stiff
3 Steering geometry incorrect

(d) Excessive tyre wear

1 Check 4 in (a); 1 in (b); and 3 in (c)

(e) Rattles

1 Axle arms lubrication neglected or worn bearings
2 Damper mountings loose
3 Stabilizer brackets loose

NOTES

CHAPTER 7

REAR AXLE ASSEMBLY AND HUBS

7:1 General description

. Referring to **FIG 7:1**, the rear axle consists of a tubular crossmember on each end of which trailing tubular arms are pivoted on taper roller bearings and carry the rear hubs and brake backplates. As described in **Chapter 8**, a common interacting spring unit connects each pair of arms, front and rear, on each side of the vehicle. Telescopic dampers are provided in later models.

7:2 Removing and refitting the axle assembly

Operations to remove and refit the axle arms and crossmember are as follows:

1 Raise the vehicle as described for the front axle in **Chapter 6** and remove the wheel on the side under attention.
2 Disengage the telescopic damper (see **FIG 7:2**) by removing the two castellated nuts 1.
3 Identify the existing adjustment of the suspension tie rod by paint marks 2 (see **FIG 7:3**) on the V-pivot carrier or link and on the threaded end of the tie rod. Slacken the tie rod, remove one of the clips 4, hold the axle arm and remove the V-pivot 3.

4 Dismantle the brake pipe assembly shown in the lower view in **FIG 7:3**. Unscrew the two union nuts 7 on the pipes leading from the three-way union 6 on the lefthand side of the car or the single nut of the righthand side. Remove the nut 5 securing the assembly to the chassis.
5 Remove the dust shield from the arm and then the adjusting nut (see **FIG 7:4**), taking out the splitpin and using the tool No. 1833.T.
6 Disengage the arm from the crossmember, tapping it off with a mallet if necessary.
7 If required, remove the inner bearing and the felt or rubber oil seal, using the special puller tool No. 1829.T as shown in **FIG 7:5**. Prise out a felt seal with a screwdriver, otherwise attach the puller behind the rubber seal to extract the seal and bearing together.
8 Removal of the crossmember if necessary involves firstly the removal of a rear wing and then the fuel tank from its connections with the chassis and the crossmember. Removal of the latter can now be performed by releasing the four retaining bolts 4 (see **FIG 7:6**), the double link 3 under the bolt heads and the aluminium distance piece 2 between the

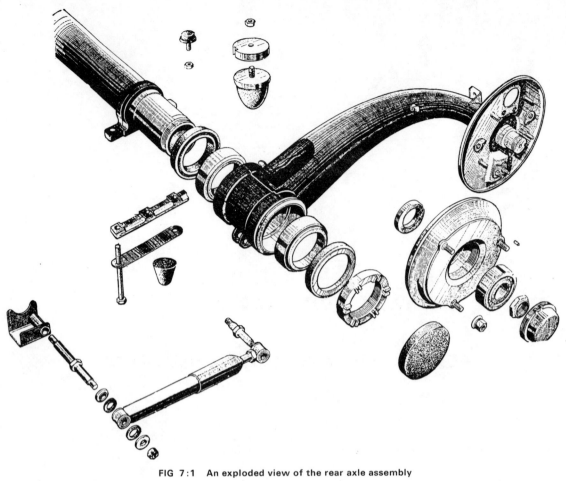

FIG 7:1 An exploded view of the rear axle assembly

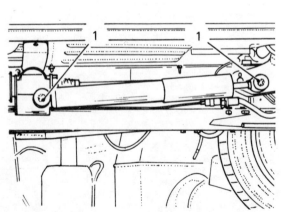

FIG 7:2 Rear damper attaching nuts shown at 1

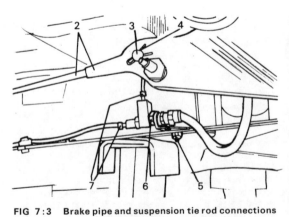

FIG 7:3 Brake pipe and suspension tie rod connections

Key to Fig 7:3   2 Paint markings   3 V-pivot   4 Clip
5 Nut   6 Three-way connection   7 Union nuts

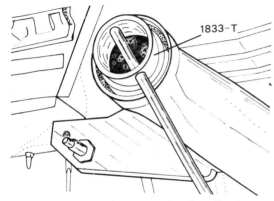

FIG 7:4 Removing the rear arm bearing adjusting nut

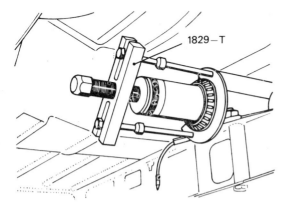

FIG 7:5 Removing the inner bearing

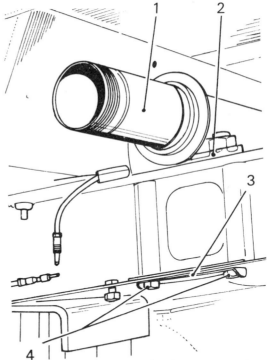

FIG 7:6 Details of attachment of rear crossmember

Key to Fig 7:6   1 Crossmember   2 Aluminium support
3 Securing link   4 Bolts

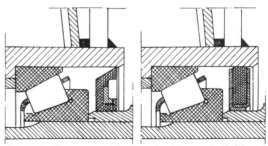

FIG 7:7 Correct positioning of rubber seals (left) and felt seals (right)

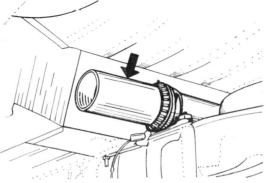

FIG 7:8 Fitting the inner bearing

crossmember and the chassis. When refitting, ensure that the dowels in the crossmember and the support 2 are firmly engaged.

Vehicles fitted with front disc brakes have brake pipes coiled inside the rear crossmember and these must be removed before the rear arms can be detached. Removal of the crossmember end cover will reveal the pipe which is removed by unscrewing the wheel cylinder union and three-way fixture fitted to the crossmember. It is necessary to remove the fuel tank. The pipe is retained by a stud which is pushed into the crossmember after removal of the nut. Clips hold the pipe to the trailing arm.

Refit the axle assembly by following the dismantling operations in reverse, with attention given to the following details:

1 Use new felt or rubber seals when refitting the inner bearing, locating them in the positions shown in **FIG 7:7** with a tube (arrowed in **FIG 7:8**).

2 Continue the assembly of the outer bearing and the tubular arm as described for the front axle assembly in **Chapter 6**.

3 Refit the telescopic dampers (if fitted) with the components shown in **FIG 7:9**. Tighten the nuts 11 to a torque of 2.4 kgm and fit new splitpins. Bleed the brakes as described in **Chapter 10**.

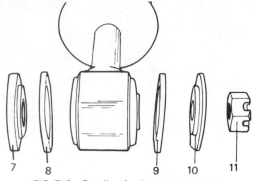

FIG 7:9   Details of a damper mounting

Key to Fig 7:9
8/9 Anti-noise rings
7 Shouldered thicker washers
10 Shouldered washers   11 Nut

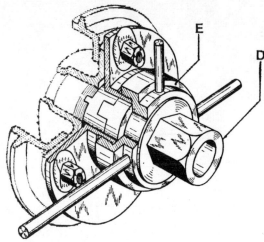

FIG 7:11   Removing or refitting the hub ring nut

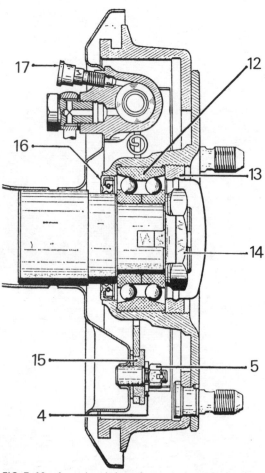

FIG 7:10   A sectional view of a rear hub and brake drum

Key to Fig 7:10
4 Washer   5 Cam nut
12 Bearing outer race   13 Ring nut   14 Spindle nut
15 Brake shoe nut   16 Seal   17 Bleed screw

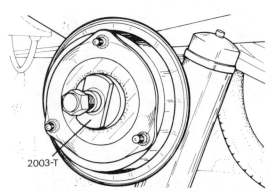

FIG 7:12   Removing a rear brake drum

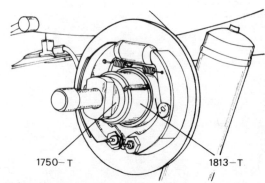

FIG 7:13   Extracting a bearing inner cage with the tools shown

7:3 Rear hub removing and refitting

To remove a rear hub, raise the vehicle as previously described and remove the wheel. Proceed as follows:

1 Referring to **FIG 7:10**, drill out the peened metal locking the ring nut 13. Hold the brake drum with a lever against the wheel studs and remove the ring nut with the aid of the tools Nos. 3301.T and 3304.T shown in **FIG 7:11**. Fit the assembly on the wheel studs and screw in the nut E without tightening it. Lock the part D by inserting the pin, then unscrew the ring nut by turning the hexagon on D.

2 Remove the nut 14 retaining the bearing and then remove the brake drum using the extractor tool No. 2003.T (see **FIG 7:12**). The inner cage of the bearing may remain on the spindle and can be extracted by the tools Nos. 1750.T and 1813.T as shown in **FIG 7:13**. Drive out the outer race 12 and the seal 16.

3 When reassembling, fit the seal with the lip towards the bearing. The seal must not rub against the bearing and a clearance of 1 to 1.5 mm should be obtained.

4 Press the two bearing inner races together with a bolt and two washers and check the play on the bearing. Coat the latter with an approved grease and press it into the bore of the hub with a tube of inside diameter 72 mm and outside diameter 75.5 mm against the outer race.

5 Adjust the brake shoes (see **Chapter 10**), tighten the nuts and fit new splitpins.

6 Locate the brake drum on the spindle and press on the bearing inner case with a tube of inside diameter 36.5 mm and outside diameter 44 mm. Fit a new bearing nut and tighten it to a torque of 27 to 30 kgm. Peen the collar of the nut into the spindle groove.

7 Fill the ring nut cover with approved grease and fit the nut with the tools as used for removal and described in Operation 1. Tighten the nut to a torque of 35 to 40 kgm and peen over the metal in two places. Refit the wheel and lower the vehicle to the ground.

7:4 Fault diagnosis

(a) Wheel wobble

1 Worn hub bearings
2 Uneven tyre wear
3 Loose wheel fixings

(b) Noisy axle

1 Lubrication neglected
2 Worn pivot bearings
3 Damper mountings loose
4 Dampers not working

NOTES

CHAPTER 8

FRONT AND REAR SUSPENSION

8:1 General description
8:2 Adjusting ground clearance
8:3 Removing a suspension cylinder
8:4 Dismantling and reassembling a suspension
      cylinder

8:5 Refitting a suspension cylinder
8:6 Lubrication
8:7 Inertia dampers
8:8 Fault diagnosis

8:1 General description

The main suspension elements consist of compression spring units (see FIG 8:1) in cylinders centrally situated longitudinally on each side of the vehicle and attached by tie rods to each axle arm. Upward movement of a wheel on the arm at either front or rear compresses the appropriate spring through its tie rod, the springs reacting against the ends of the common housing and with interaction between front and rear. Additional damping devices are provided on some cars by means of oil-filled inertia dampers on each wheel serving to damp out the unsprung weight, as well as friction-type dampers on each front axle arm (see Chapter 6) with telescopic dampers (see Chapter 7) at the rear, or in later Ami and Dyane models telescopic dampers at both front and rear.

8:2 Adjusting ground clearance

To measure the ground clearance the vehicle should be on a flat level surface with the tyres inflated to their correct pressure, the spare wheel and tool kit on board and 5 litres of fuel in the tank. Otherwise the vehicle should be in running order with the front wheels in the straightahead position and no other load carried.

Measurements are made between the ground and the underside of the chassis at a point halfway between the heads of the two crossmember securing bolts (see FIG 8:2). If fitted, remove the anti-roll bar clamps on the lefthand side. The protective covers of the front friction dampers where fitted should be removed and the securing nuts of telescopic dampers loosened. Prior to measurement, rock the vehicle in order to settle the suspension. Clearances should be as follows:

	Front (mm)	Rear (mm)
Ami 8	187.5 to 192.5	277.5 to 282.5
Ami 8 Estate . .	192.5 to 197.5	287.5 to 292.5
AK Van	209.5 to 214.5	344.5 to 349.5
Dyane and 2CV	192.5 to 197.5	277.5 to 282.5

Adjust if necessary by screwing the suspension tie rods in or out until the correct clearance is obtained (see FIG 8:3). The use of the special tools shown is advised, as grips or wrenches could leave marks on the rods which would lead to their failure. Hold the suspension cylinder by hand when adjusting as if it turns it would affect the adjustment on the other tie rod. Shake the tie rods and recheck the adjustments at both ends on completion. Finally, adjust the clearance of the rear end of the

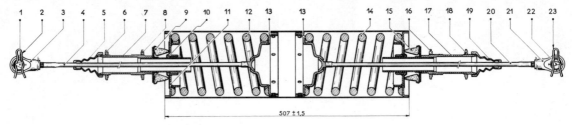

FIG 8:1 A sectional view of a suspension cylinder

Key to Fig 8:1 1 V-pivot 2 Clip 3 Tie rod screwed end 4 Front tie rod 5 Dust cover 6 Outer nut of adjustable sleeve 7 Adjustable sleeve 8 Inner nut of adjustable sleeve 9 Rubber buffers 10 Felt washer 11 End cover 12 Spring 13 Compression caps 14 Spring 15 Rubber buffers 16 Inner nut of adjustable sleeve 17 Adjustable sleeve 18 Outer nut of adjustable sleeve 19 Dust cover 20 Rear tie rod 21 Tie rod screwed end 22 V-pivot 23 Clip

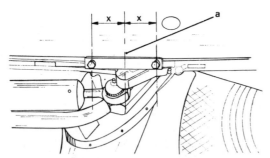

FIG 8:2 Point of measurement of ground clearance

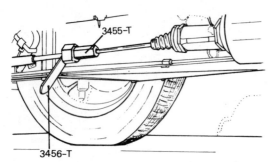

FIG 8:3 Adjusting front ground clearance

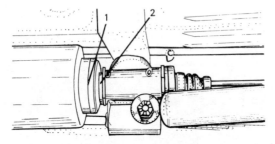

FIG 8:4 Play of 2 mm to be set between the rubber buffer 1 and the sleeve 2

cylinder and the flexible stop to give a play of 1 mm on the Ami saloon and 2 mm on all other vehicles (see FIG 8:4). Check that the rubber stop buffers on the chassis at the front (see FIG 8:5) have a clearance 'a' of between 3 and 6 mm from the arm connections. Adjust if necessary with shims between the rubber buffers and their supports.

8:3 Removing a suspension cylinder

To remove a suspension cylinder, raise the vehicle and fit firm stands. Operations are as follows:
1 Remove the damper(s) (see **Chapter 7**) and remove the stabiliser bar where fitted. Disconnect the suspension tie rods.
2 Disconnect the boots 5 and 19 (see **FIG 8:1**) from the sleeves 7 and 17.
3 On vehicles equipped with friction dampers, hold each sleeve 7 with the tool No. 3458.T (see **FIG 8:6**). Unscrew completely the inner nuts 8 at front and rear, for which the spanner No. 3453.T is available. Disengage the sleeves from their attachment on the longitudinal member and withdraw the cylinder assembly by passing the tie rods through the apertures provided in the supports.
4 On vehicles equipped with hydraulic dampers, fully unscrew the inner nut 8 of the front sleeve and the outer nut 18 of the rear sleeve, using the tools previously mentioned. Remove the rear tie rod end 21, then disengage the rear sleeve from its support to withdraw the cylinder assembly towards the front, directing the rear tie rod through the supporting fixture.

8:4 Dismantling and reassembling a suspension cylinder

Dismantling a cylinder is undertaken as follows:
1 Unscrew the ends of the tie rods 3 and 21 (see **FIG 8:1**). Disengage the boots 5 and 19, the sleeves 7 and 17, the nuts 8 and 16 and the rubber stops 9 and 15.
2 Mark with a scriber the angular position of the end cap with relation to the housing.
3 Referring to **FIG 8:7** grind off the welding at c, then withdraw the assembly of the tie rod 4, the cover 11, the spring 12 and the compression cap.

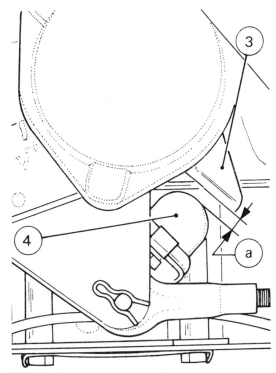

FIG 8:5 Showing clearance of 2 mm required at a between the rubber buffer 4 and the arm stop 3

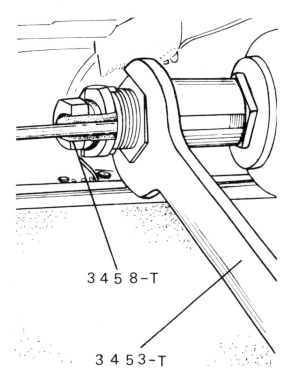

3 4 5 8 – T

3 4 5 3 – T

FIG 8:6 Showing the tools used for dismantling the suspension cylinder

4 When reassembling, soak the caps in castor oil for about 15 minutes. Do not grease the linings. Note that the front of the cylinder is marked 'AV'.

5 Reassemble by following the dismantling operations in reverse. Reweld the front end cover on the cylinder.

8:5 Refitting a suspension cylinder

Refitting operations are as follows:

1 For vehicles with friction dampers, locate the inner nuts 2 (see **FIG 8:8**) against the rubber buffers.

2 Engage the tie rods in the chassis supports through the apertures f.

3 Engage the front sleeve with the chassis support and tighten the outer nut 4 to obtain a minimum distance a (see **FIG 8:9**) of 12 mm, leaving one or two threads at b behind the inner nut 2. Lock this nut with the tools described in Operation 3 in **Section 8:3**.

4 Mount the rear sleeve and provisionally tighten the inner and outer nuts.

5 For vehicles with hydraulic dampers, proceed as in Operation 1 then locate the rear tie rod in the chassis support and the front tie rod in the aperture f provided in the front support.

6 Mount the front sleeve on the chassis. Tighten the nuts and continue as in Operations 3 and 4.

7 Reassemble the tie rods and end connections, applying some engine oil to the V-pivots. Lower the car to the ground and adjust the ground clearances as described in **Section 8:2**.

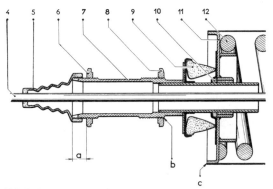

FIG 8:7 A sectional view of part of a suspension cylinder

Key to Fig 8:7   4 Tie rod   5 Dust cover   6 Outer nut   7 Sleeve   8 Inner nut   9 Rubber buffer   10 Felt washer   11 End cover   12 Spring   a, b, c See text

8:6 Lubrication

Raise the vehicle on firm supports and disengage the rubber dust covers 5 and 19 (see **FIG 8:1**). Hold the sleeves to unscrew only the inner nuts 8 and 16 with the tools previously described. The outer nuts 6 and 18 are not loosened so as not to alter the existing ground clearances. Disengage the sleeves 7 and 17 from their chassis supports.

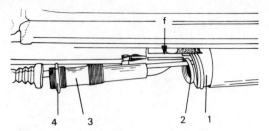

FIG 8:8   Reassembling the suspension cylinder components

Key to Fig 8:8   1 Rubber buffer   2 Inner nut   3 Sleeve
4 Outer nut   f Access aperture

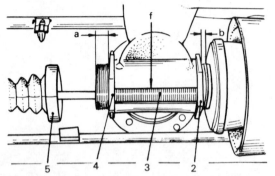

FIG 8:9   Reassembling the suspension cylinder components

Key to Fig 8:9   2 Inner nut   3 Sleeve   4 Outer nut
5 Dust cover   a, b, f See text

Inject castor oil into the cylinder with the aid of a syringe about 400 mm long, then refit the components removed for access. Lower the vehicle to the ground and carry out a road test of about 50 km. If noise persists it will be necessary either to fit a new unit complete or to overhaul the existing one.

Knife edges:

The V-pivots, shown at 1 and 22 in **FIG 8:1**, are referred to as knife edges in certain handbooks and these have to be lubricated with engine oil every 3000 miles. It is suggested that this oil can be best applied with a small painting brush.

8:7 Inertia dampers

Removal of an inertia damper is obtained by removing the wheel and unscrewing the two nuts retaining the damper on its bracket.

Check the damper by shaking it vertically with its filler plug at the top pointing upwards. A loud rubbing noise is normal and the unit is in good condition if the weight inside can be felt to be moving. The oil may be renewed if required by removing the filler plug, draining out the oil from the body and refilling the unit with 75 cc of light machine oil. Fit the plug, and refit the unit on its bracket with the plug pointing upwards. Tighten the securing bolts to a torque of 6 kg m.

8:8 Fault diagnosis

(a) Wheel wobble

1 Worn suspension linkage
2 Loose wheel fixings
3 Uneven tyre wear
4 Worn hub bearings

(b) Bottoming of suspension

1 Rubber buffers unserviceable
2 Suspension out of adjustment
3 Ground clearances incorrect
4 Weak or broken suspension springs
5 Dampers not working

(c) Heavy steering

1 Front tyres under-inflated
2 Axle arm ball joints stiff
3 Suspension or steering geometry incorrect

(d) Excessive tyre wear

1 Check 1 in (a); 5 in (b) and 3 in (c)

(e) Rattles

1 Neglected lubrication, worn bearings or loose chassis attachments
2 Damper mountings loose
3 Stabilizer brackets loose

CHAPTER 9

THE STEERING GEAR

9:1 Operating principles and construction
9:2 Steering gear removal and refitting
9:3 Steering column assembly

9:4 Checking camber angle
9:5 Adjusting track
9:6 Fault diagnosis

9:1 Operating principles and construction

The steering gear is of the rack and pinion type, the steering rack being incorporated in the front axle crossmember (see **Chapter 6**). Details of the assembly are shown in **FIG 9:1**.

Movement of the steering wheel is transmitted by the steering shaft to a helically-toothed pinion supported by a ballbearing. Rotation of the pinion causes the rack to move laterally, when track rods attached to the rack by ball joints transmit this movement to the steering arms on each side of the vehicle and cause the road wheels to turn. On later Ami 8 models two universal joints are incorporated in the steering column to provide an inclination for improved driving comfort.

9:2 Steering gear removal and refitting

The rack and pinion steering gear can be removed from the vehicle as a unit without removing the steering column by removing the front axle arm and crossmember assembly as described in **Chapter 6**. Dismantle the gear as follows:

1 Referring to **FIG 9:2**, disconnect the track rod ball joints, for which the tools Nos. 1964.T and 3502.T

(see **FIG 9:3**) are available. Remove the rubber thrust pad, which should be renewed on reassembly.
2 Remove the slide 28 (see **FIG 9:2**), the moving cover 27 and the ball joint guides 24 and 25. Remove the rack and tube assembly from the axle crossmember.
3 Remove the nut 45 (see **FIG 9:4**) which locks the steering pinion, using tool No. 1981.T, and free the pinion from its housing. Drive out the pinion bush 42 by a shouldered mandrol inserted from inside the housing. The bush will push out the expanding plug 41.
4 Remove the splitpin and the ball joint end nut 30, for which a spanner No. 3691-3 is available. Proceed to remove the seat 31, the ball 32, the seat 33, the spring 34, the spacer 35 and the similar components 36 to 39. Clean all the parts.

Reverse these operations to refit the assembly, giving attention to the following details:

1 Smear the inside of the rack tube with an approved grease when engaging it with the guide 29. Fill the holes 'a' with grease and also grease the balls before insertion.
2 Screw in the stub nut 30, then loosen it by about one-sixth of a turn. Ensure that the ball joints turn freely

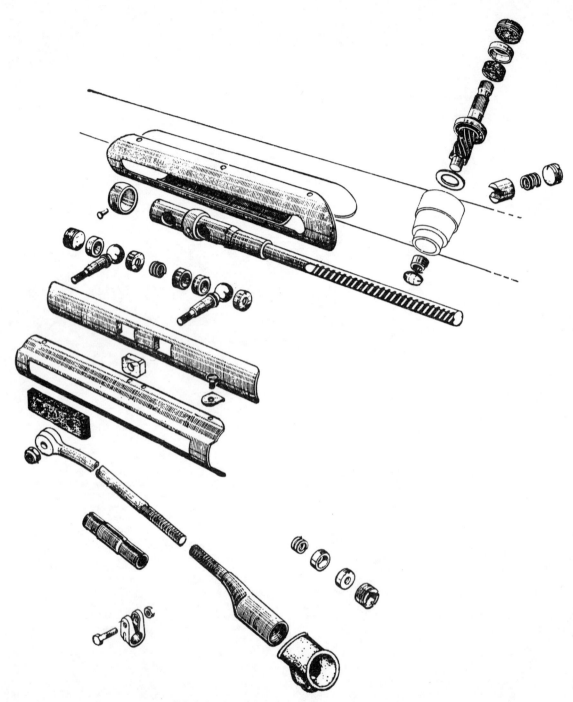

FIG 9:1 An exploded view of the steering gear

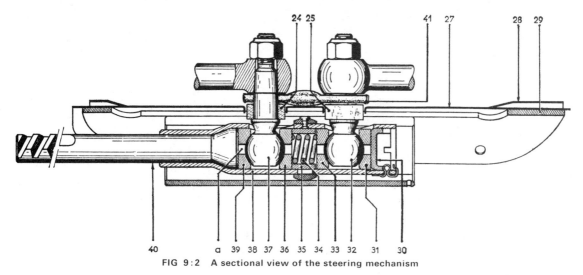

FIG 9:2 A sectional view of the steering mechanism

Key to Fig 9:2   24/25 Guides   27 Moving cover   28 Slide   29 Ball joint guide   30 End cover   31/39 Ball joint seats
32/37 Balls   33/36 Ball joint seats   34 Spring   35 Spacer   38 Tube   40 Rack   41 Rubber pad   a Lubrication hole

without any play. Fit a new splitpin in the hole in the nut nearest to one of the notches, locating the head in the notch. Turn down the arms of the splitpin on the rack sleeve so that the ends do not rub against the ball joint guide.

3 Peen the expanding plug 41 (see **FIG 9:4**) in the metal of the housing recess and fill the bush from the inside with grease.

4 Smear the outside of the rack with grease together with its tube when assembling to the axle cross-member. Grease the pinion bearing 44 and the surrounding area.

5 Fit the pinion and the felt 46 and tighten the ring nut 45 to a torque of 10 kg m with the spanner No. 1981.T.

6 Grease the friction surfaces of the moving cover 27 and locate it with its shorter end to the lefthand side of the vehicle. Fit the cover slide 28, tighten the bolt and ensure that the rack moves freely. Turn down the lockwashers.

7 After fitting the spring in its guide (see **FIG 9:4**) temporarily tighten the nut 48 and provisionally fit the steering wheel and shaft to the pinion. Turn the steering wheel to move the rack through its entire length of travel. Progressively tighten the nut 48 to

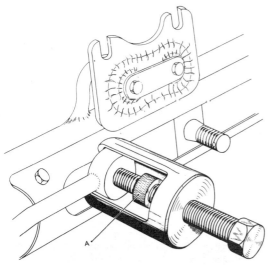

FIG 9:3 Ball joint removal tools Nos. 1964.T and 3502.T, showing the knurled tightening nut at **A**

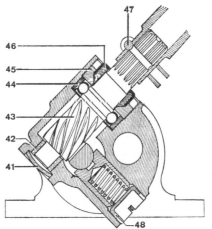

FIG 9:4 A sectional view of the pinion assembly

Key to Fig 9:4   41 Expanding plug   42 Bush
43 Pinion   44 Ballbearing   45 Ring nut   46 Felt ring
47 Screw   48 Adjusting nut

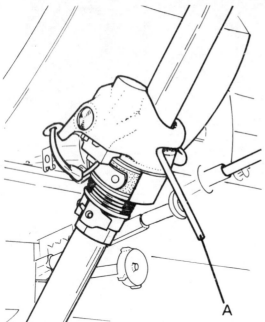

FIG 9:5 Removing the half rings on the anti-theft assembly with the Allen key **A**

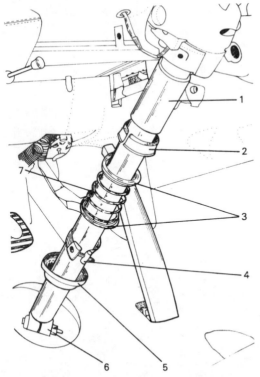

FIG 9:6 Steering column components

Key to Fig 9:6   1 Locating tube   2 Conical cup
3 Spring seating cups   4 Clamp   5 Rubber joint
6 Clamp   7 Spring

find the point of greatest resistance, if any, and adjust the pressure of the guide at this point by gradually loosening the nut. The rack should be able to be moved without feeling the action of individual teeth.

8 Complete reassembly by following the dismantling operations in reverse order, tightening the ball joint nuts to a torque of 2.5 to 3.0 kg m.

The nuts, which have a nylon insert to lock them, may be used several times provided the insert is in good condition. The nuts should be too tight on the thread to be turned by hand. When the nylon meets the thread it will cause the pin to turn, so it will be necessary to close the taper to prevent this. Do so by inserting an open-ended spanner or other spacer under the nut and tightening down. It will be found, after removal of the spacer, that the taper will hold.

9:3 Steering column assembly removal and refitting

On Ami 6 vehicles fitted with an anti-theft assembly and with no universal joints on the steering shaft, procedure to remove the steering wheel and column is as follows:

1 Remove the spare wheel. Put the wheels in the straight-ahead position and bring the mark on the rack sliding cover (see **FIG 9:8**) in line with the ball joint guide. In this position it should be possible to lock the anti-theft device if correctly adjusted. Scribe the position of the steering column in relation to the anti-theft assembly.

2 Remove the bearing cover, then remove the two bolts securing the anti-theft half rings, using a 5 mm Allen key as shown in **FIG 9:5**. The half rings will move apart and remain in the anti-theft assembly.

3 Remove the floor carpet and disengage the rubber joint 5 (see **FIG 9:6**). Unscrew the nut of the clamp 6 and take out the bolt.

4 Remove the clamp 4, the spring 7 and its seating cups 3, the conical cup 2, the locating tube 1 and the steering tube.

5 Refit in reverse order of disassembly. Engage the steering column on the pinion, positioning the steering wheel spoke at 30 deg. below the horizontal towards the right. Fit the clamp 6 and turn down the lock-washer.

6 Locate the tube 1 and compress the spring 7. When its coils are in contact tighten the clamp 4 with the spanner No. 1994.T.

7 Fit the second tightening bolt of the half rings and tighten it by a few threads. Turn the steering column to align the marks made when dismantling. Tighten the two clamp bolts alternatively to bring the half rings evenly into position.

8 If the anti-theft assembly is incorrectly positioned, with the wheels located straight-ahead turn the half rings until the anti-theft mechanism can be locked. Then mark the position of the steering column and secure the half ring bolts. Assemble the remaining items in the reverse order of their removal.

On Ami 8 vehicles with universal joints on the steering column (see **FIG 9:7**), unlock the anti-theft device, take out the bolt 12 and withdraw the steering wheel and shaft assembly 1. Lift the rubber sleeve 8, with the

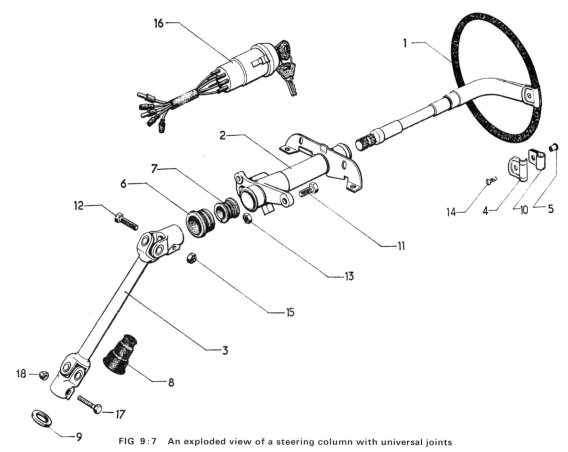

FIG 9:7 An exploded view of a steering column with universal joints

Key to Fig 9:7 1 Steering wheel and column 2 Fixed tube 3 Transmission shaft 4 Bracket 5 Screwed socket 6 Rubber joint 7 Rubber joint 8 Rubber sleeve 9 Washer 10 Bracket 11 Bolt 12 Bolt 13 Nut 14 Screw 15 Nylstop nut 16 Ignition switch and connector 17 Bolt 18 Nylstop nut

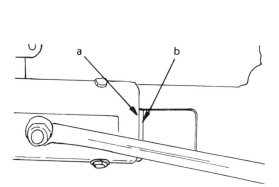

FIG 9:8 Alignment of the ball joint guide a with the mark b on the sliding cover

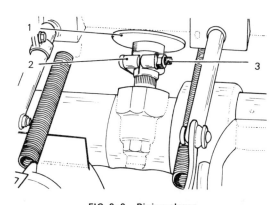

FIG 9:9 Pinion clamp

Key to Fig 9:9 1 Rubber sealing cap 2 Clamp 3 Bolt

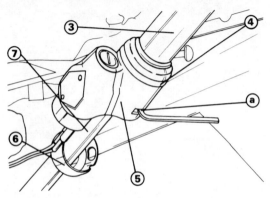

FIG 9:10 Anti-theft mechanism on 2CV models

Key to Fig 9:10   3 Fixed tube   4 Clamp   5 Anti-theft device   6 Protective collar   7 Steering column   a Aperture and Allen key

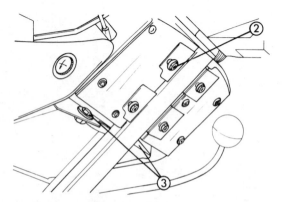

FIG 9:11   2CV column assembly showing the retaining screws 2 and bolts 3

aid of french chalk or a non-mineral grease if necessary, then remove the bolt 17 to free the transmission shaft 3.

Refit in the same way in reverse, renewing the Nylstop nuts 15 and 18. With the wheels placed straight-ahead, bring the mark 'b' (see FIG 9:8) on the steering sliding cover flush with the ball joint guide 'a' on the lefthand side. Position the steering wheel with the spoke to the right at an angle of 30 deg. below the horizontal. The wheel should be adjusted so that the spoke does not touch the plastic bush on the fixed tube 2 when the wheel is fully turned between its limits of travel. During final reassembly tighten the nuts 15 and 18 to a torque of 2 kgm.

On the 2CV the pinion clamp must be released (see FIG 9:9) and the supply leads disconnected from the anti-theft device. Free the protective collar by removing the screw on the locking device and allow the collar to slide down as shown at 6 in FIG 9:10. Unlock the anti-theft device and remove the screws at 'a' with a 5 mm Allen key as shown, to free the locking bush.

To remove the clamp 4 it will be necessary to obtain a tool such as 2412-T to release the shear nuts that retain

it. This tool is used in the same way as type 3902-T described later for the Dyane. Remove the steering column 7, fixed tube 3 and rubber support block.

Replace in the reverse order using new shear nuts. Tighten the pinion clamp nut to 1.9 kgm. When refitting the locking device only moderately tighten the screws at 'a' and check the action of the lock before tightening the screws fully.

On Dyane models the anti-theft locking ring is welded on the steering column, which cannot be removed without removing the fixed tube. Operations are as follows:

1 Remove the embellisher and the screws to withdraw the steering wheel. Disconnect the leads from the anti-theft device.

2 Remove the bolt from the retaining clamp of the rack pinion, also the bolts 2 and 3 from the supporting housing (see FIG 9:11).

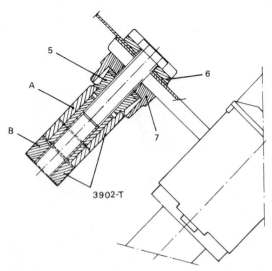

FIG 9:12   Removing the tapered screw assembly retaining the fixed tube and the anti-theft mechanism

Key to Fig 9:12   5 Tapered screw   6 Upper plate   7 Lower support   A Hexagonal body of 3902.T   B Barrel nut of 3902.T

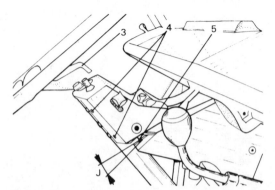

FIG 9:13   Refitting the steering wheel and column showing the embellisher 3 and the retaining bolts 4 and 5. J = .05 to .50 mm

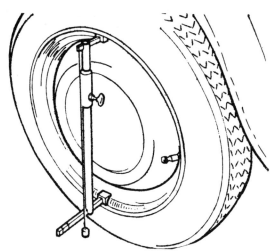

FIG 9:14 Apparatus used for wheel alignment

3 Referring to **FIG 9:12**, use the special tool No. 3902.T
to withdraw the two tapered screws 5 holding the
small upper plates 6 and the lower supports 7. The
method used is to place the assembly of the body A and
the nut B against the conical retainer 5, then screw in
the nut B on the end of the clamping device so as to
engage the bevelled edge of the hexagonal body A
in the retainer 5. The assembly is then removed by
turning the body. The construction of the conical nuts
requires their renewal on reassembly.

4 Proceed to disengage the rack pinion and the
assembly of the fixed tube and shaft, which may then
be separated. Withdraw the rubber ring and the Rilsan
ring.

5 Refit by following the foregoing operations in reverse.
The pinion clamp is fitted as described for other
models. Referring to **FIG 9:13**, locate the bolts 4 and
5 and the two conical fasteners by hand. New conical
elements are supplied with a stem and hexagonal head
which are designed to break off when the required
fastening torque has been applied.

6 Insert the plate and support 6 and 7 (see Operation 3).
Centralize the column assembly of fixed tube and
shaft as far as allowed by the play of the steering
pinion, then tighten the conical elements without
breaking off the stems. Shims are available to provide
a required play 'J' of between .05 and .50 mm
between the upper support and the dashboard before
fully tightening the bolts 5. Then tighten the latter and
the bolts 4.

7 Fit the steering wheel and the embellisher 3 and check
the anti-theft device operation and the rotation of the
steering column. Finally tighten the conical elements
holding the plate and support 6 and 7 to the fixed
tube and the anti-theft device until the stems break
off leaving the conical heads in position. Connect the
leads to the anti-theft device.

9:4 Checking camber angle

Checks on the correct alignment of the front wheels
can be undertaken by service agents equipped with the
apparatus shown in **FIG 9:14**. The wheel inclination

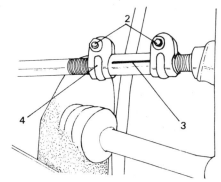

FIG 9:15 Track rod adjustment details, showing the
bolts 2, the sleeve 3 and the collars 4

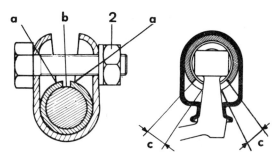

FIG 9:16 Location requirements at a, b and c for
securing a track rod adjusting clamp with the bolt 2

is checked either in the straight ahead position, using
the mark on the steering rack cover as described in
Section 9:3 or at full lock. If the steering rack cover is
not marked, the required position can be obtained by
lining up each front wheel with a cord stretched at wheel
centre height over the length of the vehicle. The apparatus
when positioned as shown in the illustration has a plumb
line which descends upon a scale marked with the
designed requirements for individual vehicles.

9:5 Adjusting track

The front wheels are set slightly outwards, with a
difference between front and rear of between 1 and 3 mm.
This setting can be checked in service workshops using
proprietary equipment or somewhat less accurately by
ordinary measurement. For the latter, both front tyres
must be inflated to the correct pressure with the car on
level ground and the underbody heights correctly
adjusted (see **Chapter 8**). Measure the distance between
the outer edges of the wheel rims at wheel centre height
at the front. Mark these two points of measurement and
then roll the car forward for exactly half a revolution of
the wheels so that the marks finish up at the rear.
Measure again the marked points. If this distance is
smaller by 1 to 3 mm the adjustment is correct.

If otherwise, the track rods must be adjusted with the
rack ball joints located in the middle of their travel. This
is done by aligning the mark on the steering rack
cover as described in **Section 9:3**. On each track
rod loosen the nuts 2 (see **FIG 9:15**) in the clamps

on the sleeves 3 and turn each sleeve as required to alter the track rod lengths. Each sleeve must be turned by the same amount to obtain the required wheel alignment. Retighten the securing nuts with the collars 4 located as shown in the illustration. Ensure that the points 'a' (see **FIG 9:16**) are not positioned in the slot 'b' of the sleeve and that the ball joints have clearances as shown at 'c'.

9:6 Fault diagnosis

(a) Wheel wobble

1 Unbalanced wheels or tyres
2 Slack steering connections
3 Incorrect steering geometry
4 Excessive play in steering gear
5 Worn hub bearings

(b) Wander

1 Check 2, 3 and 4 in (a)
2 Uneven tyre pressures
3 Uneven tyre wear
4 Weak dampers

(c) Heavy steering

1 Check 3 in (a)
2 Very low tyre pressures
3 Neglected lubrication
4 Wheels out of track
5 Steering gear maladjusted
6 Steering column bent or misaligned
7 Ball joints tight

(d) Lost motion

1 Worn ball joints

CHAPTER 10

THE BRAKING SYSTEM

10:1 Description of layout

Up to late 1978, only Ami versions had disc brakes fitted on the front wheels. Then, a dual-circuit braking system with front discs was introduced on the Dyane. With both drums and discs, the front brakes are located inboard on the differential shafts and the rear brakes on the wheel hubs. All brakes are operated hydraulically by a pendant pedal (see **FIG 10:11**) suspended from a bracket under the dashboard, which operates a master cylinder conveying hydraulic fluid under pressure to operating cylinders on front and rear brakes. An early layout of the brake system is shown in **FIG 10:1**. Later modifications include the substitution of the rear brake hoses by an assembly of spiral pipes located in the rear crossmember.

Adjusters are provided on drum brake backplates to compensate for lining wear, so that the brake shoes can be moved nearer to the brake drum. Disc brakes where fitted have two pistons, one on each side of the disc, to compress the pads against the disc when hydraulic pressure is applied. The disc brakes are self-adjusting, the operating pressure automatically compensating for wear of the pad lining materials.

A cable-operated handbrake acts on the front wheels with independent pad arrangements incorporated in disc brakes. A safety lock is provided in the brake handle as shown in **FIG 10:2**. The brake is released by pulling the handle upwards, then pressing the button 2 and pushing the handle fully forwards. To apply the safety lock, pull out the button 2 and turn it until the tongue T enters one of the notches provided for its retention. Release the lock by returning the tongue to the notch 3.

10:2 Routine maintenance, brake shoe adjustment

The level of the brake fluid in the transparent reservoir should be inspected and topped up if necessary at least every 5000 km or 3000 miles. The reservoir is fitted on the lefthand side of the engine compartment and on Ami 6 and 8 vehicles the removal of the spare wheel is necessary to gain access. The reservoir is marked at the level to which fluid should be filled and which should not be exceeded. Wipe the cap before and after removing it and ensure that the vent hole is clear. Extreme cleanliness is essential for the efficient operation of the system. It is also most important that **the correct approved fluid** is used, as a change or mixture of fluids

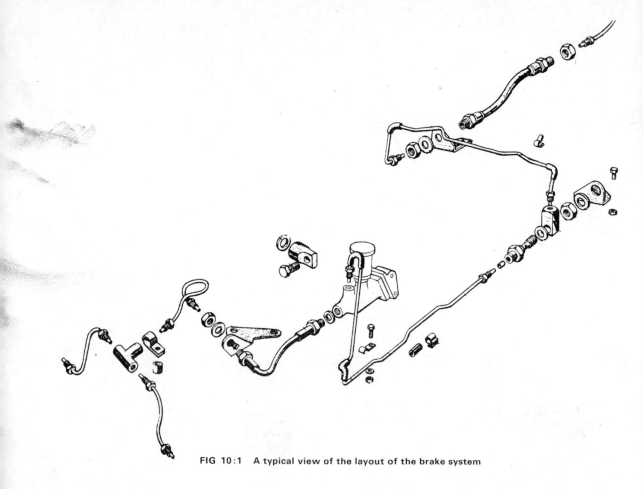

FIG 10:1   A typical view of the layout of the brake system

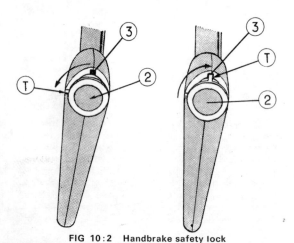

FIG 10:2   Handbrake safety lock

Key to Fig 10:2   2 Button   3 Slot   T Locking tongue

can quickly damage the seals and cup washers in the system. The recommended fluids are Lockheed 55 for vehicles with drum brakes at front and rear and the green LHM mineral fluid for Ami 8 and Dyane 6 vehicles with disc brakes at the front.

Adjustment of drum brakes should be carried out every six months or at other times as necessary. Each brake shoe is adjusted individually by the cams shown in **FIG 10:3**. Raise the front or rear of the vehicle and turn the cams in the direction of the arrows with a 13 mm spanner. At the same time rotate the drum by hand. When the drum stops release the adjuster and once again turn until the shoes just make slight contact. **This adjustment should never end with a releasing motion.** Carry out the same operations on the other wheel or wheels fitted with drum brakes and lower the vehicle to the ground. As previously mentioned, front disc brakes, where fitted, are self-adjusting.

10:3 Brake pads and brake shoe linings

Brake pads and brake shoe linings should be inspected for wear and the drums blown clear with compressed air every six months. Brake pads should be renewed when worn down to a lining thickness of 4 mm, measured between the contact face of the disc and the face of the

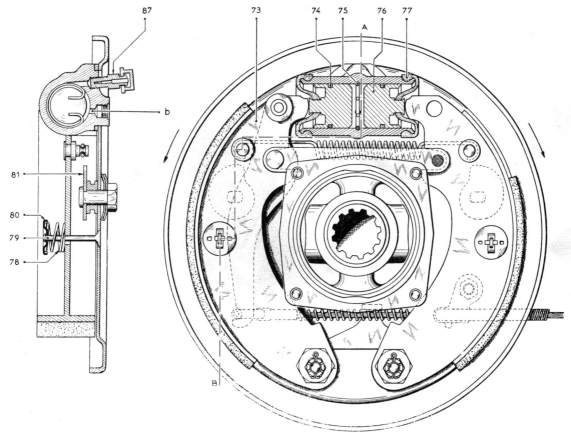

FIG 10:3   A sectional view of a drum brake

Key to Fig 10:3   73 Brake shoe   74 Sealing rings   75 Circlip   76 Piston   77 Boot   78 Spring   79 Guide rod   80 Spring retaining cap   81 Adjusting cam   87 Bleedscrew   Dotted lines show cams and handbrake lever

brake pad support plate. The reservoir should not be replenished immediately prior to fitting new brake pads, as the insertion of new pads will cause a return of fluid so that the reservoir may overflow. Brake pads are renewed as follows:

1 Referring to **FIG 10:4**, push the pads 3 apart with a clamp or pliers, taking care not to apply pressure on the disc but on the caliper bosses.

2 Pull out the ends 'c' of the double spring 5, push the pad downwards and withdraw it from the front.

3 Fit the new pads by locating them in the caliper and pushing them towards the rear as far as possible. Secure by fitting the spring 5 into the notch 'd'. Check the pedal travel as described in **Section 10:8**.

4 In the case of the handbrake pads, release the handbrake to its fullest extent and remove the brake caliper (see **Section 10:7**).

5 Remove the pads 14 and loosen the nut securing the cams 18. Fit the new pads, using a piece of rubber between them to prevent them falling out and ensuring that the anti-rattle springs are in position.

6 Refit the caliper and proceed to adjust the pad clearances. Position the cams 18 with the notch 'e' facing upwards and ensure that the levers 15 are in

contact with their stops.

7 Turn the cams 18 to obtain a clearance of .1 mm between the pad 14 and the lug 'f' on the lever 15.

8 Adjust each cam in turn and tighten the bolts 25 to a torque of 4 kg m, ensuring that the cams do not rotate while tightening. Adjust the handbrake cable as described in **Section 10:8**.

Dyane brakes are of similar design, but with the caliper reversed for easier handbrake adjustment.

Brake shoes on drum brakes should be relined if the linings are worn down to the extent that the rivets are likely to contact the drum or if they show signs of contamination from grease or oil. Renewal is preferably to be undertaken by fitting new shoe assemblies complete with linings. To ensure even braking it is necessary to renew the brake linings on both front or both rear wheels at the same time and also to check that the drum surface finish is similar on each side. Renewal of linings on front drum brakes is undertaken as follows:

1 Referring to **FIG 10:5**, detach the drive shaft 6 from the brake drum 5, as described in **Chapter 5**. Remove the flexible heating tube 2 including the attaching components 1 and 4 and the shutter control rod 3, then withdraw the brake drum.

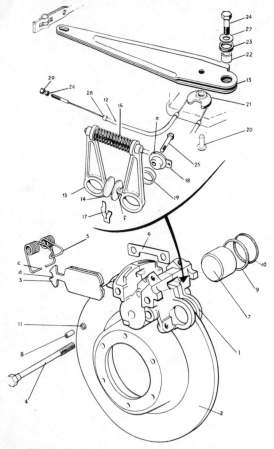

FIG 10:4   An exploded view of a disc brake

Key to Fig 10:4   1 Caliper   2 Disc   3 Pad   4 Caliper
rear bolt   5 Double spring   6 Adjusting shim   7 Piston
8 Connecting pipe   9 Seal   10 Seal   11 Ring seal   12 Cable
13 Swivel lever   14 Pads   15 Levers   16 Lever return spring
17 Anti-rattle springs   18 Cams   19 Sleeve   20 Spindle
21 Cable guide   22 Sleeve   23 Washer   24 Bolt   25 Bolts
26 Nut   27 Washer   28 End fitting   29 Locknut   c Spring
ends   d Notch   e Notch   f Lug

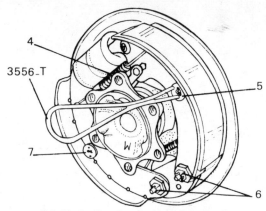

FIG 10:6   Details of a front drum brake

Key to Fig 10:6   4 Return spring   5/7 Guide rod spring
caps   6 Pivot nuts

2 Turn the adjusting cams (81 in **FIG 10:3**) to pull back
the brake shoes, disconnect the brake pipe and remove
the two retaining bolts to take off the wheel cylinder.

3 Remove the splitpins and take off the nuts 6 (see
FIG 10:6) retaining the shoe hinge cams. Remove the
thrust spring caps 5, turning them a quarter of a turn
to disengage them from the guide rods (79 in **FIG
10:3**). Use either a forked tool as in the illustration or
circlip pliers. Remove the guide rods and the springs.

4 Unhook the handbrake cable then withdraw the brake
shoes from their pivot pins, tilting the rear shoe upwards. Remove the return spring 4.

5 Reverse the foregoing operations to refit the shoes or
fit new ones. Reconnect the handbrake cable to the
shoe 3 (see **FIG 10:7**) and the return spring with the
longer end on the same shoe. A new spring should be
fitted.

6 Before refitting the drum the brake shoes should be
centralized, as described in the following Section.
Complete refitting by reassembling the components
removed for access. Adjust the brakes (see **Section
10:2**) and bleed the system as described in **Section
10:9**.

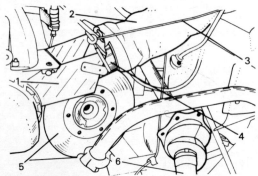

FIG 10:5   Removing a front brake drum

Key to Fig 10:5   1 Heater housing   2 Flexible conduit
3 Shutter control   4 Spring   5 Drum   6 Drive shaft

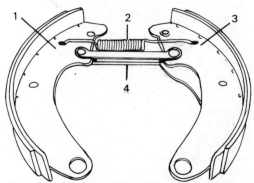

FIG 10:7   Brake shoes, front drum brake

Key to Fig 10:7   1/3 Shoes   2 Return spring   4 Link

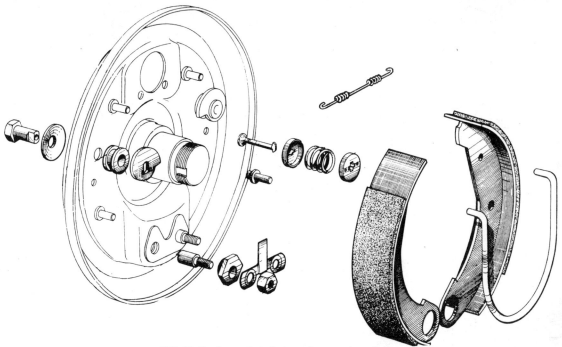

FIG 10:8 An exploded view of a rear drum brake

Renewal of linings on rear drum brakes is undertaken by first removing the drum as described in **Chapter 7**. Components of a rear drum brake are shown in **FIG 10:8** and operations are similar to those performed on front drum brakes. Remove the thrust spring caps or seats and withdraw the shoe locating springs. Unhook the U-shaped return spring with a screwdriver and remove the nuts from the pivot pins. Disengage the flat washers, the cams and the brake shoes. On reassembly, centralize the brake shoes (see **Section 10:4**) and refit the remaining components in the reverse order of their disassembly. Adjust the brakes (see **Section 10:2**) and bleed the system as described in **Section 10:9**.

10:4 Centralizing brake shoes

For the correct location of the front brake shoes a special tool is used as shown in **FIG 10:9**. Procedure is to adjust the cam on one shoe so that the lining is just touching the drum, turning the drum to allow for any eccentricity. Remove the drum. The gauge is then located on the drive flange and secured in place with the retaining nut. The pointer A is placed against the top of the brake shoe and for the correct centring of the shoes the pointer should lightly touch the lining during rotation. Adjustment is made by the adjusting cams and the pivot cams 1. Readjust the brakes on completion.

A similar procedure is undertaken for centring the rear brake shoes, using the gauge No. 3555.T as shown in **FIG 10:10**.

10:5 Instructions on servicing hydraulic internals

Absolute cleanliness must be observed in all operations concerned with hydraulic components. In particular,

when carrying out any work on the hydraulic system it must be ensured that only clean approved brake fluid is used to top up or refill the system. Note that different fluids are used depending upon whether drum brakes or disc brakes are fitted on the front wheels. For drum brakes the approved fluid is Lockheed 55 but for disc brakes the green mineral LHM fluid must be used. With the LHM fluid petrol is used for cleaning the hydraulic components concerned and **only the LHM fluid** should be used for their lubrication when fitted. Where the Lockheed 55 fluid is specified, however, **do not use mineral oils** or cleaning fluid extracted from mineral oil such as petrol, paraffin or carbon tetrachloride and clean the parts with methylated spirits or the approved fluid. Observance of these requirements is essential, as departure from them

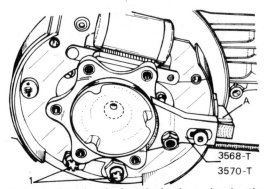

FIG 10:9 Centring the front brake shoes, showing the gauge pointer **A** and the pivot bolts 1

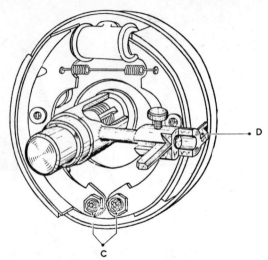

FIG 10:10 Centring the rear brake shoes with the gauge No. 3555.T, showing the pointer **D** and the pivot cam nuts **C**

could affect the seals and soon render the brakes inoperative.

It is inadvisable to re-employ brake fluid which has been extracted from the system during overhaul or bleeding operations. Aeration may persist and it may also be contaminated by traces of solvents in the container used or by particles of dust and grit. Pistons and piston seals should be kept away from any possibility of picking up grease or oil. Never replace hydraulic seals that have been used, always fit new seals from a service kit. Immerse all hydraulic components in clean approved brake fluid when reassembling.

When removing or refitting hydraulic connecting hoses they must not be twisted or permanent damage will result. Always unscrew the union nuts on the metal pipes first.

Hold the hexagon on the flexible hose with a second spanner as a precaution against its turning when removing or fitting a hose locknut at a bracket.

10:6 Removing, servicing and refitting master cylinder. Wheel cylinders

Details of the master cylinder and its pedal connection are shown in **FIG 10:11**. To remove the master cylinder, remove the spare wheel and proceed as follows:

1 Empty and remove the fluid reservoir 1 (see **FIG 10:12**). Unscrew the union 2 of the rear brake pipe connection and the unions 3 and 4 retaining the outlet hose. Observe the requirements in the last paragraph of the preceding Section.

2 Remove the floor covering, disconnect the clutch cable at its pedal connection, unhook the accelerator control from its pedal and disconnect the stoplight switch leads. Remove the three bolts indicated in **FIG 10:13** and the four bolts to the rear of the master cylinder, to release the pedal gear.

3 Disengage the pedal and master cylinder assembly from inside the vehicle. Take out the splitpin and remove the spindle. Remove the two securing bolts to free the master cylinder. New spacers will be required on reassembly.

Overhaul of the master cylinder can be undertaken without detaching it from the pedal assembly. Operations are as follows:

1 Referring to **FIG 10:14**, remove the circlip 7 and the pushrod 8 after withdrawing the splitpin and the spindle 9.

2 Continue to withdraw the end washer 6, the piston 4 and cup 5, the cup 3, the return spring 2 and the check valve 1.

3 Clean the components with fresh brake fluid, observing the instructions given in **Section 10:5**. Ensure that the piston and cylinder bore are undamaged and that the main and compensating ports are undamaged.

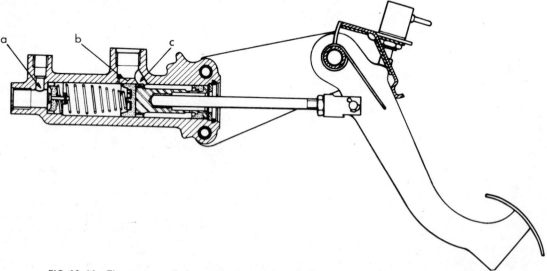

FIG 10:11 The master cylinder and brake pedal assembly, showing the fluid ports a, b and c

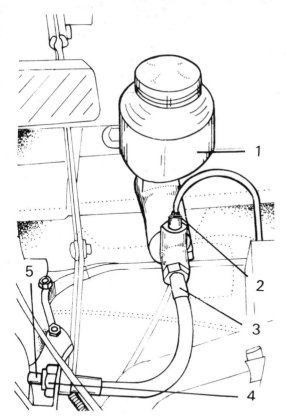

FIG 10:12 The fluid reservoir, master cylinder and pipe connections

Key to Fid 10:12   1 Reservoir   2 Rear brake pipe union
3 Hose union   4 Locknut   5 Union

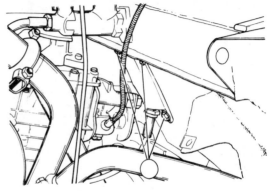

FIG 10:13   Pedal assembly bolts

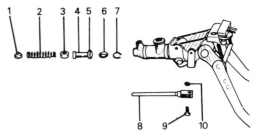

FIG 10:14   An exploded view of the master cylinder

Key to Fig 10:14   1 Check valve   2 Return spring   3 Cup
4 Piston   5 Cup   6 End washer   7 Circlip   8 Pushrod
9 Spindle   10 Washer

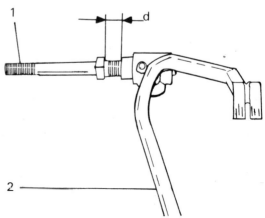

FIG 10:15   Assembling the shaft 1 to the accelerator
pedal 2   d=10±.25 mm

The filler cap vent must be free from obstruction. Renew the main and secondary cups, check valve and check valve washer.

4 For reassembly, smear the cylinder bore and all components with the recommended brake fluid. Assemble the components in the reverse order of their removal. Insert the main cup 3 lip foremost and do not turn back or damage the lip. The lip of the secondary cup 5 should face the front of the piston. Finally, compress the spring, engage the end washer and circlip and reassemble the pushrod.

When refitting the master cylinder assembly, locate the shaft 1 (see FIG 10:15). in the accelerator pedal 2 to obtain a clearance 'd' of 10±.25 mm. Subsequent operations are the reverse of those undertaken when dismantling. Tighten the securing bolts on the dash panel and insert the clutch cable stop between two of the lower bolts. On completion, fill the reservoir with the approved fluid, bleed the system and adjust the pedal height (see Section 10:8).

The method of overhaul is similar for the master cylinder used when front disc brakes are fitted. FIG 10:16 shows a cross section of the assembly. The screw 2 must be removed before extracting the pistons. Note that the two seals 5 and 8 are not identical. Ensure the holes a, b and c are not obstructed.

An alternative type of master cylinder used is shown in FIG 10:17. To dismantle this it is necessary to remove the roll pin shown. A 3 mm diameter drill held horizontally in a vice will do this if the cylinder body is fitted so that the drill enters the pin. The body must be turned clockwise and pulled backwards to disengage the pin.

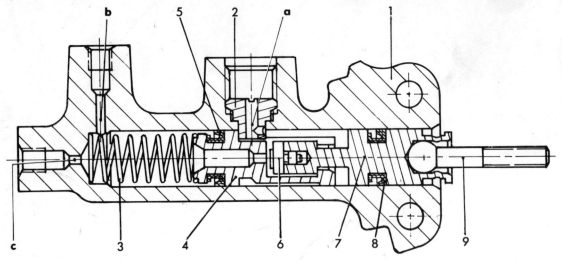

FIG 10:16 The master cylinder used when front disc brakes are fitted

Key to Fig 10:16   1 Body   2 Screw   3 Spring   4 Primary piston   5 Primary cup   6 Valve   7 Thrust piston
8 Thrust cup   9 Pushrod

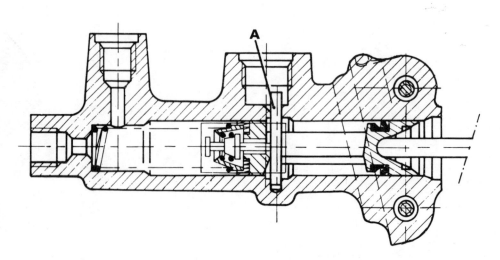

FIG 10:17 Alternative type of master cylinder showing the roll pin 'A'

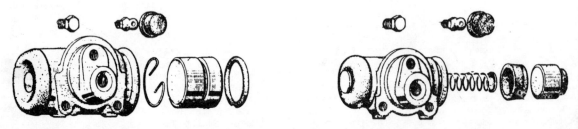

FIG 10:18 Exploded views of the wheel cylinders

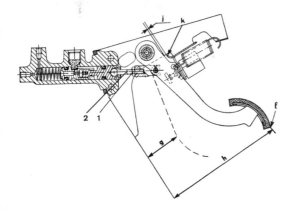

FIG 10:19 A sectional view of the master cylinder and brake pedal assembly on vehicles with front disc brakes, showing the locknut 1 and pushrod 2. Dimensional details are given in text

The details of the wheel cylinders shown in **FIG 10:18** will guide dismantling and overhaul operations, which are undertaken as described for the master cylinder in the previous instructions.

10:7 Dismantling and reassembling brakes

Operations needed for the dismantling and reassembly of drum brakes are described in **Section 10:3**. The procedure to be followed for disc brakes is as follows:

1 Disconnect the battery and remove the heater connections. Remove the starter motor, which can be rested on one side without disconnecting the leads

2 Remove the main brake pads as described in **Section 10:3**. Disconnect the brake pipes and plug them to avoid loss of brake fluid.

3 Remove the caliper rear securing bolt 4 (see **FIG 10:4**), then slacken the front securing bolt about half a turn to allow the assembly to be tilted towards the front. Refit the bolt 4 in the caliper halves and fit a nut (10 mm diameter × 150) to retain the halves together before removing the front bolt completely. Disconnect

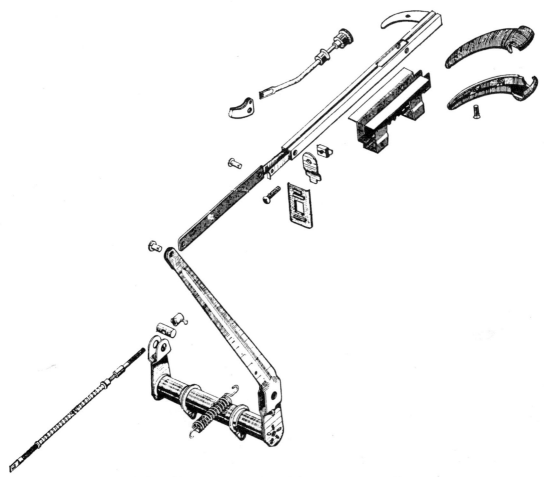

FIG 10:20 An exploded view of the handbrake assembly

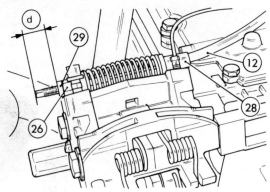

FIG 10:21   Adjusting the handbrake cable

Key to Fig 10:21   12 Cable sheath   26 Adjusting nut
28 Cable end   29 Locknut

the handbrake cable and remove the assembly from the vehicle.

4 Continue dismantling by removing the bolts 25, the cams 18, the levers 15, the return springs 16 and the handbrake pads 14. Remove the nut to separate the two halves.

5 Remove the spring 5 retaining the pads 3, the shim 6, the connecting pipe 8 and the ring seal 11.

6 From each of the two half-housings remove the anti-rattle spring 17 and then the piston 7 by blowing compressed air into the brake fluid inlet port. Take care that the piston is not ejected sharply. Remove the seals 9 and the bleed screw on the righthand caliper.

7 Clean the caliper bores, seal grooves and fluid channels with brake fluid, noting the precautions to be taken mentioned in **Section 10:5**. Inspect the pistons for scores or other defects.

8 Use a dial gauge to test the run-out of the disc, which should not exceed .2 mm. If otherwise there are six alternative positions for locating the disc, one of which may bring the run-out within the specified limit. If still not obtained the disc should be refaced or renewed.

9 Reassemble the caliper by reversing the dismantling operations, smearing the seals with the special LHM brake fluid. Fit the adjusting shim 6 removed when dismantling and tighten the securing bolts 4 to a torque of 4.5 to 5.0 kg m. Ensure that the mating faces are clean and free from scores when refitting the caliper. Refit the brake pads according to the details given in **Section 10:3**. Connect and adjust the handbrake cable and reconnect the brake hose, assembling it so that it is free from twist. Bleed the brake system as described in **Section 10:9**.

Note that since October, 1969, the brake discs have been cooled by air from two ducts connected by pipes to the main air cooling system. The disc cooling ducts are secured to the gearbox housing at the front and to the silencer retaining bolts at the rear.

10:8 Brake pedal and handbrake adjustment

On disc brake models, referring to **FIG 10:19**, pull the pedal fully upwards, when there should be a clearance 'j' of 2 mm between the pedal and the support at 'k'.

Adjust, if necessary, by slackening the locknut 1 and altering the effective length of the pushrod as previously described. Also with the pedal fully raised the distance 'h' should be 125 ± 2.5 mm. Adjust, if necessary, by bending the support at 'k'. With the pedal fully depressed there should be a minimum clearance 'g' of 45 mm. On Dyane cars, the caliper is reversed.

On drum brake models brake pedal adjustment is made by slackening the pushrod locknut and screwing the pushrod in or out to obtain a maximum clearance of .5 mm between the end of the pushrod and its contact with the master cylinder piston. Retighten the locknut at this position. The pedal should have a free movement (measured at the pad) of 5 mm. The distance between the pad and the floor (as at **h** for disc brakes) should be 120 ± 5 mm for the Ami or 130 ± 5 mm for other vehicles.

Details of the handbrake control are shown in **FIG 10:20**. On drum brake models, raise the front of the vehicle and adjust the two cables in turn by means of the wing nuts to obtain a light braking action at the third notch of the handbrake lever and locking of the wheels on the fifth notch. On Ami models with disc brakes, ensure that the end fittings 28 (see **FIG 10:21**) and cable covers 12 are in position. Turn the nuts 26 as required to obtain the application of the brake on the third and fifth notches of the handle travel as previously described. The length 'd' of the screwthreads is to be equal on both sides to within the nearest 5 mm.

10:9 Bleeding the system

Bleeding is undertaken as follows:

1 Clean the areas around the bleed valves and top up the fluid reservoir. Use only the specified brake fluid as instructed in **Section 10:5** and add additional fluid progressively as the operations proceed. Ensure the vent-hole in the reservoir cap is clear.

2 Remove the cap from the righthand rear bleed nipple and fit a bleed tube, preferably of a transparent type. Place the other end of the tube in a glass jar containing a small quantity of the approved brake fluid. During the bleeding operation the end of the tube must be kept immersed in the fluid.

3 Unscrew the bleed valve about half a turn, depress the brake pedal fully and then allow it to return to its off position. Brake fluid and/or air should have been pumped into the jar; if not, unscrew the bleed valve further. Pause about three seconds to allow full recuperation of the master cylinder.

4 Continue depressing the brake pedal, pausing after each return stroke, until the fluid entering the jar is clean and free from air bubbles. Press the pedal down to the floor and hold it there whilst the bleed valve is tightened. Do not overtighten and keep the master cylinder topped up with approved fluid during the operation.

5 Remove the tube and refit the dust cap. Bleed the remaining brakes in the same way. Note that where disc brakes are fitted, only one nipple is fitted at the front. This is on the righthand caliper. On conclusion it is advisable to repeat the operation on the rear brake initially bled to check that air has not been drawn in through the master cylinder. Finally, top up the reservoir, refit the cap and road test the brakes.

It should be noted here that brake fluid is harmful to the paintwork of the car and care should always be taken to ensure that it is not spilled on the panels. In the case of the plastic panels used on Mehari vehicles, any spillage of brake fluid should be washed off immediately with white spirit.

10:10 Fault diagnosis

(a) 'Spongy' pedal

1 Leak in system
2 Worn master cylinder
3 Leaking wheel cylinders
4 Air in the system
5 Gaps between shoes and underside of linings

(b) Excessive pedal movement

1 Check 1 and 4 in (a)
2 Excessive lining wear
3 Very low fluid level in supply reservoir
4 Too much free movement of pedal

(c) Brakes grab or pull to one side

1 Brake backplate loose
2 Scored, cracked or distorted drum or disc
3 High spots on drum
4 Unbalanced shoe adjustment
5 Wet or oily linings
6 Worn steering connections
7 Mixed linings of different grades or unchamfered ends
8 Uneven tyre pressures
9 Broken shoe return springs
10 Seized handbrake cable
11 Disc brake caliper piston sticking

(d) Brakes dragging

1 Check 2, 4 and 11 in (c)
2 Incorrect adjustment of master cylinder pushrod
3 Master cylinder piston sticking
4 Wheel cylinders sticking

NOTES

CHAPTER 11

THE ELECTRICAL EQUIPMENT

11:1 The system, exchange units, test equipment

A 12-volt electrical system with negative earth return is used in Ami vehicles since 1966, superseding a previous 6-volt system. The 12-volt system also applies to Dyane 6 models, but early Dyane 4 models are equipped with the 6-volt system. With the latter system a DC generator or dynamo of the two-brush type is incorporated in the end of the crankshaft, but with the 12-volt system a separate AC generator or alternator is used. Both types of generator charge the battery, which in turn supplies the electrical energy to operate the starter motor, the ignition (see **Chapter 3**), the lights and other accessories, of which the general arrangement is shown in the wiring diagrams in the Appendix. The alternating current in the later type of generator is converted into direct current for charging the battery through silicon diodes. These are in the nature of one-way valves which prevent the current being returned to the alternator under low voltage conditions.

Major mechanical and electrical defects in the generator, starter motor and other integral features of the system are best remedied by fitting new units on an exchange basis, but instructions are given on adjustments which can be undertaken with some basic understanding of electrical theory and practice and without elaborate equipment. The wiring diagrams will assist in identifying and tracing wiring faults. Electrical adjustments, however, require precise measurement and an accurate voltmeter and ammeter should be available. In the absence of a voltmeter a useful item of equipment is a test lamp, consisting of a small 6-volt or 12-volt bulb in a holder with two well-insulated leads ending in crocodile clips. If one lead is earthed, the bulb will light if the other lead is connected to any terminal or point in the system which is 'live'.

11:2 Battery maintenance and testing

Regular attention is necessary to keep the battery in good working order and to extend its life. The top of the battery should be kept clean and dry. Any signs of corrosion may be removed by a weak solution of ammonia and hot water. The terminals should be coated with petroleum jelly and anti-sulphuric paint may be used for adjacent parts such as battery bolts and support.

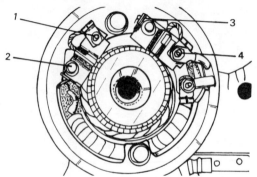

FIG 11:1 A view of the generator commutator and brushes, showing the retaining screws 1 to 4

If the electrolyte level is less than about 5 mm above the plates, distilled water should be added. Should leakage or spilling require the addition of dilute sulphuric acid of the correct specific gravity it can usually be obtained already diluted. But if strong sulphuric acid is used, remember **when diluting always to add acid to water** and on no account add the water to the acid.

The condition of the battery can be checked by specific gravity tests. Test the specific gravity of the electrolyte in each cell with a hydrometer, when for an electrolyte temperature of 16°C (60°F) readings as follows should be obtained. The readings should be corrected by adding or subtracting .002 for each 3°C (5°F) rise or fall from that temperature.

Cell fully charged	1.270 to 1.290
Cell half discharged	1.190 to 1.210
Cell fully discharged	1.110 to 1.130

Where an alternator is employed, both the positive and negative leads must be disconnected when charging the battery. Under normal operating conditions the alternator output is sufficient to keep the battery charged, but if the car is not used for a long period of time it is good practice to include a monthly charge.

DC GENERATOR

11:3 Generator maintenance, electrical tests in situ

As the generator is driven directly by the crankshaft, maintenance is mainly concerned with servicing or renewing the brushes when required. This involves disconnecting the battery and the removal of the fan, the front shell and grille as described in **Section 1:7** in **Chapter 1**.

Test the brushes for freedom of movement in their holders, gently moving the brushes by pulling on their connectors. If the movement is sluggish, remove the brush from its holder and ease the sides by slightly polishing them with a smooth file. If the brushes are worn below 8 mm in length new brushes must be fitted. Referring to **FIG 11:1**, remove the nut 1 or the nut 4 for the brush under attention. Disengage the spring to remove the brush. Hold up the spring 2 or 3 and assembly the new brush, then refit the nut 1 or 4. Note that the output terminal is connected under the nut 4. Finally, refit the items removed for access.

To test the output of the generator first make sure that the output and field terminals on the generator are correctly connected to their respective terminals on the regulator as shown in the wiring diagram. Operations are then as follows:

1 Disconnect the wires from the output and field terminals of the generator and join the terminals together with a short piece of wire.

2 Connect a 0-20 voltmeter between this junction and earth. Run the engine at a fast idling speed when the voltage reading should rise rapidly without fluctuation. Conduct the test as quickly as possible, as the fan is absent and the engine is running without cooling. Also avoid increasing the engine speed or the generator may be damaged.

3 If there is no reading, check the generator leads, brushes and brush connections. If the reading is very low, the field or armature windings may be at fault.

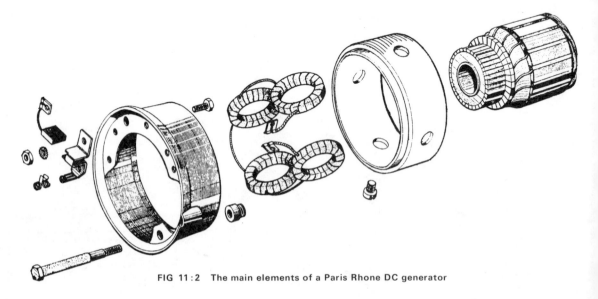

FIG 11:2 The main elements of a Paris Rhone DC generator

4 If the generator is in good order, leave the temporary link in position between the terminals and restore the original connections correctly. Remove the output lead from the regulator and connect the voltmeter between this lead and a good earth. Run the engine as before, when the reading should be the same as that measured directly on the generator. No reading indicates a break in the cable from generator to regulator. Repeat the test on the field cable and finally remove the temporary link from the generator.

Regulators of either Ducellier or Paris Rhone manufacture are connected to the generator to control the output charge to the battery. The charging rate will be high when the battery is discharged and low when the battery is fully charged, independent of the speed of rotation of the generator. The regulators fitted include three units, i.e., a voltage regulator, a current regulator and a cut-out unit. The latter is an electro-magnetic switch which breaks the circuit when the generator voltage falls below that of the battery, so preventing the discharge of the battery through the generator. Defects in this apparatus are uncommon, but electrical tests can be carried out if required by a service agent with the necessary facilities and experience.

11 : 4 Removal and servicing

The main elements of a Paris-Rhone DC generator are shown in **FIG 11 : 2**. Ducellier generators are also employed and are similar except for minor differences of design such as the shape of the field coils. Removal and overhaul of either type of generator is undertaken as follows:

1 Disconnect the battery earth lead and remove the fan, the grille and the surrounding shell, as described in **Chapter 1**.

2 Referring to **FIG 11 : 3**, disconnect the red and yellow leads 2 and 3 from the outlet and field circuit terminals. Remove the two generator securing bolts 1 and disengage the generator from the casing, taking care not to pull on the brush holders. The tool No. 2205.T (see **FIG 11 : 4**) is used to remove the armature from the crankshaft.

3 Inspect the brushes as previously described. Examine the surface of the commutator, which should be smooth and free from pitting or burned spots. Clean it with a cloth moistened with petrol. If this is ineffective, carefully polish it with a strip of glasspaper, not emerycloth, while the armature is rotated. If the commutator is badly worn or scored it may be faced up in a lathe with a very sharp tool, using a shouldered mandrel to maintain the centring of the commutator in line with the crankshaft. The original diameter must not be reduced by more than 2 mm. If necessary, undercut the insulation between the segments after rectification to a depth of .8 mm with a hacksaw blade ground down to the thickness of the insulation. Then polish the commutator with fine glasspaper and remove all copper dust. Check the circuit to earth with a simple bulb circuit.

11 : 5 Refitting

1 Clean the tapered seat in the armature and the mating surface on the crankshaft with petrol or methylated spirits. Check the generator housing in the crankcase.

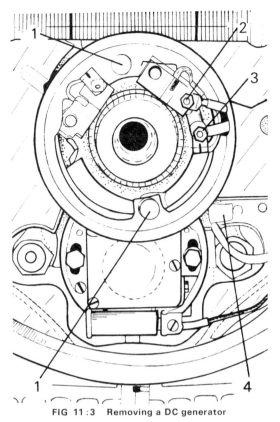

FIG 11 : 3   Removing a DC generator

Key to Fig 11 : 3   1 Retaining bolts   2 Output terminal (red wire)   3 Field terminal (yellow wire)   4 Cable holder

2 Locate the armature on the crankshaft. Raise the brushes and hold them by their springs as shown at 'a' in **FIG 11 : 5**.

3 Lightly grease the crankcase bore and engage the body of the generator. Insert the two retaining bolts 1 (see **FIG 11 : 3**) with their insulators, tightening them first by hand and then to a torque of .5 to .8 kg m. Do not overtighten to avoid damaging the brush plate bosses. Lower the brushes into contact with the armature.

4 Connect the leads to the terminals 2 and 3, inserting serrated washers and tighten the screws. Retain the leads by the clip 4 and other retainers on the crankcase and the generator body.

5 Refit the fan and other items removed for access.

ALTERNATOR

11 : 6 Description and operation

The advantages of an AC alternator in the electrical system instead of the conventional DC generator are that the alternator can operate at higher speeds than the DC generator and consequently improved performance is obtained at engine idling speeds. Also there is no commutator to require attention and regulation is simplified by providing an instrument only for voltage control.

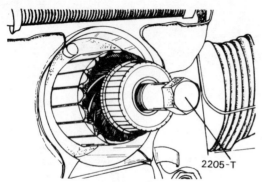

FIG 11:4 Withdrawing the armature

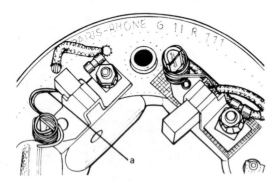

FIG 11:5 Supporting the brushes at a during reassembly

Dismantling and overhaul operations on the alternator call for special experience and test equipment, especially for electronic details, and although the general procedure is described it is advised that such work should be undertaken by a qualified service agent. Details of a Ducellier alternator are shown in **FIG 11:6**. The Paris Rhone type is constructed on the same lines but with differences of design of individual components. The unit consists mainly of a rotor 8, a stator 9, a slip ring end shield 10 with two rectifying diodes, a drive end shield 5 and a pulley 3. The current is generated with a stationary armature and a revolving field system, The stator and rotor are housed between the drive and slip ring end shields, the whole assembly being secured by bolts. Two brushes are mounted on the slip ring end shield and bear on the two smooth slip rings. The slip rings replace the commutator on DC generators and because there is no interruption of current to cause sparking the alternator can run at higher speeds. The alternating current generated is rectified, or changed to direct current, by means of the silicon diodes also contained within the slip ring end shield. These diodes do not allow the return of current from the battery to the alternator windings and hence the normal cut-out on DC generators is not required. A fuse element in series with each diode is provided to interrupt the circuit in the event of the diode becoming shortcircuited. The rotor carries the excitation

winding which receives the feed through the slip rings and the brushes.

The main purpose of the regulator (see the wiring diagram) is to keep the output voltage of the alternator within defined limits which is achieved by varying the excitation of the alternator. The regulator base plate must be carefully earthed.

11:7 Testing

Whenever work is undertaken on an alternator charging system **care must be taken** as follows to avoid serious damage to the diodes:

1 All alternator systems have negative earth and the leads of the battery must never be reversed, otherwise the diodes will be burned out and the wiring possibly damaged.

2 Battery leads, or any wires in the charging system, must not be disconnected whilst the engine is running.

3 Disconnect the battery leads if charging the battery from an outside source.

4 The alternator must never be run with the output disconnected, not without the safeguard of a battery connected in the charging circuit.

5 Never check the unit by shortcircuiting either the positive terminal and earth or the excitation terminal and earth.

6 As semi-conductors are liable to damage by excessive heat, soldering or unsoldering the diode connections must always be undertaken by holding the connecting wires with pliers to act as a heat sink. The operation must be carried out as quickly as possible.

7 The alternator must be disconnected if any arc welding operations are to be performed on the vehicle.

8 Resistance readings in the components of the alternator are to be taken only with instruments that operate at a maximum of 8 volt. To check the diodes, use the operating power source.

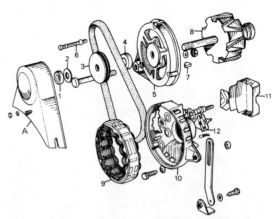

FIG 11:6 An exploded view of a Ducellier alternator

Key to Fig 11:6 1 Nut 2 Washer 3 Pulley 4 Spacer 5 Drive end shield and bearing assembly 6 Retaining screws 7 Woodruff key 8 Rotor 9 Stator 10 Slip ring end shield and bearing assembly 11 End cover 12 Brush carrier A Belt cover

9 The regulator should never operate without being earthed, otherwise the regulator windings will be destroyed.

Faults in the charging system are first to be sought in the condition of the battery, defective wiring connections or the loose adjustment of the driving belt. If the alternator is then suspect, proceed as follows:

1 Connect an ammeter in series on the output circuit.
2 Disconnect the excitation cable at the alternator to cut off the excitation circuit.
3 Using a separate cable, connect the alternator excitation to the positive terminal of a battery for the full feed (13 or 14 V) of the excitation circuit.
4 Check the driving belt tension and run the alternator at the speeds shown in the following table, according to type, just for the time required to obtain the current reading. If the current reading gives a result not far away from the values indicated the alternator is working correctly and the fault lies in the regulator circuit.

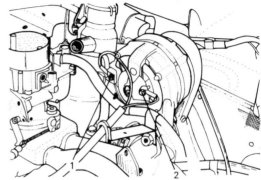

FIG 11:7 Showing the alternator field terminal 1 and output terminal 2

Alternator	Test voltage	Alternator speed rev/min	Engine speed rev/min	Output amp
Ducellier 7542.G	13V	2700	1250	7.5
Ducellier 7532.A	14V	1900	1100	6
Paris Rhone A.11.M6	14V	4200	2350	22
Ducellier 7534.A	14V	8000	4500	28
Paris Rhone A.11.M4	14V	2400	1350	8
Paris Rhone A.11.M5	14V	5400	3000	32

Testing the regulator normally requires the experience and equipment of a service agent, but the procedure is as follows:

1 Disconnect the negative terminal of the battery and the outlet lead (black) from the terminal (see **FIG 11:7**) of the alternator.
2 Connect an ammeter in series and a rheostat in parallel in the charging circuit. The required connections are (a) the ammeter positive terminal to the alternator terminal 1 (b) the ammeter negative terminal to the disconnected outlet lead (black) (c) the rheostat terminals between the ammeter negative and earth.
3 Connect a voltmeter in the excitation circuit, i.e., the voltmeter positive to the regulator terminal 3 (violet, see **FIG 11:8**) and the voltmeter negative to earth.
4 Reconnect the battery negative terminal and run the engine slowly.
5 Accelerate the engine to about 2500 rev/min (2200 rev/min in later Dyane vehicles after 1970) and adjust the rheostat to obtain an output of 15 amp or other amperage according to regulator type as given in the following table.

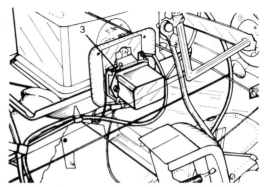

FIG 11:8 The regulator, showing the terminal 3

Regulator	Alternator speed rev/min	Engine speed rev/min (approx.)	Test temperature	Output amp	Voltage
Ducellier 8347.C	5000	2500	20°C	15	14–14.6V
Paris Rhone AYA.213	5000	2500	20°C	0–10	13.1–14.4V
Paris Rhone AYA.215	5000	2500	20°C	Above 10	12.7–14V

6 Stop the output by disconnecting for a very short time, then wait till the engine has regained its specified speed and at this moment the voltmeter should give a reading of 14 to 14.6V or otherwise as shown in the table. Note that these figures relate to an ambient temperature of 20°C. If the temperature rises the

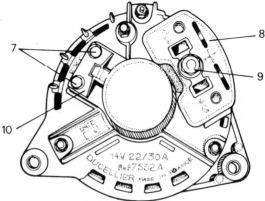

FIG 11:9 Details of a Ducellier alternator

Key to Fig 11:9
8 Plastic cover   9 Nut   7 Screws securing the brush carrier   10 Brush carrier

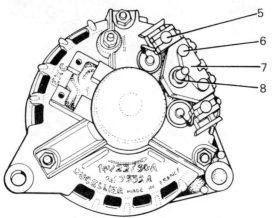

FIG 11:10   Details of a Ducellier alternator

Key to Fig 11:10   5 Diode output connections   6 Screws
7 Fuse link   8 Nut

voltage will diminish by approximately .2V for each
10°C, and vice versa. If the voltage figures are not
within the specified limits the regulator should be
renewed.

11:8 Removal, dismantling and refitting

Removal and dismantling of the alternator are undertaken as follows:

1 Disconnect the battery and the leads from the
alternator terminals. Slacken the mounting bolts and
nuts and disengage the drive belt from the pulleys.
Remove the bolts and lift off the alternator.

2 On the Ducellier type, remove the bolt 9 (see **FIG
11:9**) and the plastic cover 8. Remove the two nuts 7
to remove the brush assembly 10.

3 Remove the two retaining screws 6 (see **FIG 11:10**)
and the nut 8 to disengage the fuse link 7. Remove the
two nuts 5 from the diode connections.

4 Referring to **FIG 11:11**, remove the three bolts 6
retaining the assembly. Mark the assembly of the
front and rear bearing assemblies 5 and 10 relative to
each other and separate them together with the rotor 8
and the pulley 3. Disengage the stator 9.

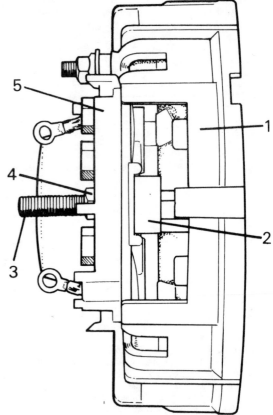

FIG 11:12   Alternator slip ring end shield

Key to Fig 11:12   1 End shield and bearing assembly
2 Insulator   3 Output terminal   4 Nut   5 Support plate

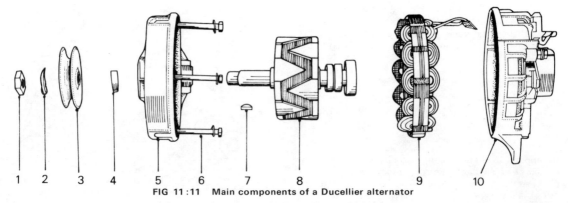

FIG 11:11   Main components of a Ducellier alternator

Key to Fig 11:11   1 Nut 2 Washer 3 Pulley 4 Spacer 5 Front bearing assembly 6 Assembly retaining bolts 7 Woodruff
key   8 Rotor   9 Stator   10 Rear bearing assembly

5 Remove the pulley by using an old belt in the pulley groove with the loose part held in a vice to hold the pulley whilst unscrewing the nut 1. Disengage the washer 2, the pulley 3, the woodruff key 7 and the spacer 4. Withdraw the rotor 8 from the bearing 5.

6 At the slip ring end, take off the nut 4 (see **FIG 11 :12**) and remove the output terminal 3 with its Teflon insulator from the inside of the end shield 1. Disengage the support plate 5.

7 The diodes may be checked by connecting a test lamp between the positive terminal of a 12V battery and the end shield 1. Connect the negative terminal of the battery in turn to each of the output terminals of the two diodes, when the lamp should light. If the battery

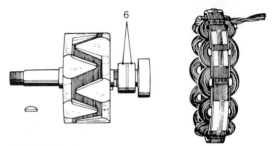

FIG 11 :13 Alternator rotor and stator windings, showing the slip rings 6

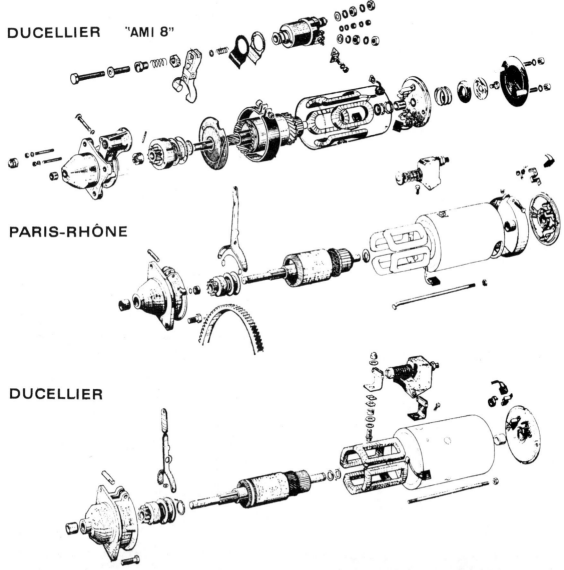

DUCELLIER "AMI 8"

PARIS-RHÔNE

DUCELLIER

FIG 11 :14 Typical details of starter motors. Top, Ducellier; centre, Paris Rhone; bottom, Ducellier

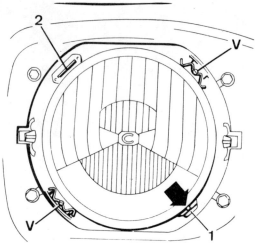

FIG 11:15 Cibie type headlamp with embellisher removed, showing: 1 Release spring, 2 Slot, V Adjusting screws

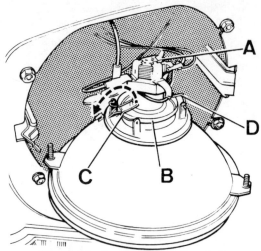

FIG 11:17 Renewing a headlamp bulb

Key to Fig 11:17 A Connector B Bulb collar C/D Springs

connections are now reversed the lamp should not light. If these requirements are not met the end shield assembly 1 should be renewed complete.

8 The stator winding insulation may be checked by applying a voltage of 110V with a 110V test lamp inserted between a green lead and earth and then between a red lead and earth. If the insulation is satisfactory the lamp should not light, otherwise it will become necessary to renew the stator.

9 The rotor winding insulation may similarly be checked under a 110V load by connecting a test lamp between a slip ring (see FIG 11:13) and earth, when the lamp should not light. If it does the rotor must be renewed.

10 The resistance between the two slip rings should be 7 ohm at 20°C. Inspect the condition of the rings,

clean them with petrol and polish them if necessary with very fine abrasive paper. Inspect the condition of the brushes and service them as necessary (see Section 11:3).

11 Reassemble and refit the alternator by following the dismantling and removal operations in reverse. Adjust the driving belt by moving the alternator on its mountings to obtain a belt tension which will allow it to be depressed approximately 12 to 13 mm midway between the pulleys.

11:9 The starter motor

The starter motor may be of either Ducellier or Paris Rhone manufacture. The main operating features of each are similar although differences exist in internal design. Starters of each make include two basic drive systems. The positive manual drive type, which is used on earlier cars in the range, and the pre-engaged, or solenoid type which are fitted to later cars. These latter are claimed to be more silent in operation and to have better lasting qualities. Some examples are shown in FIG 11:14.

In the contact switch starter, or positive manual drive starter, the starter lever is displaced by cable and spring. Integral with the fork, the lever meshes and unmeshes the pinion and the ring gear, and associated with the contact switch energizes the starter at the end of travel. In the solenoid drive starter, when the starter switch is closed the solenoid is energized and the pinion drive moves forwards, causing the pinion to engage with the ring gear on the flywheel. The armature starts turning slowly until at the end of the solenoid stroke the starter receives full current and turns the engine. Release of the starter switch enables the solenoid to withdraw the gear and disconnect the supply to the motor, with the aid of a freewheel arrangement in the Ducellier type or an armature braking device on the commutator end bracket in the Paris Rhone motor.

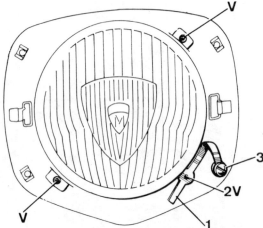

FIG 11:16 SEV type headlamp with embellisher removed, showing the release strap 1, the screw 3 and the adjusting screws V

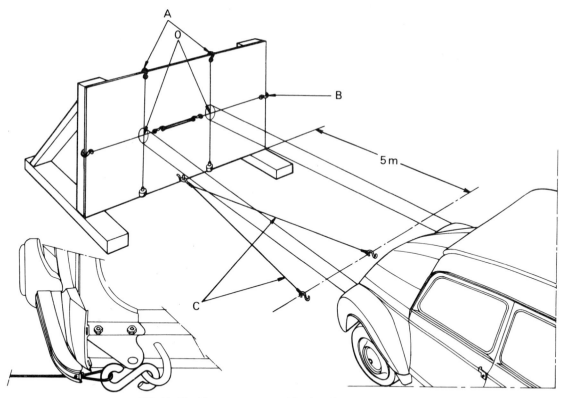

FIG 11:18   The apparatus used for headlamp beam setting

The starter may be removed by disconnecting the leads from the battery and from the starter terminals, removing the control cable end clamp or disconnecting the leads from the switch terminal according to type and removing the starter securing bolts. Check that the armature shaft is free to rotate in the brushes without binding. For a free speed check, hold the starter body in a vice and connect it to a 6 or 12 volt battery, according to the voltage system, using heavy gauge cables to carry the current required. One cable goes to the starter terminal and the other to the starter body. The starter should now run at high speed. If it does not, further tests may be undertaken by a service agent using one of several different types of testing equipment available. The brushes can be inspected if the commutator end cover is removed. Examine for wear and for freedom in their holders. All four brushes should be renewed if any are pitted or worn to one-half their original length.

Starter motors are generally reliable units which give very little for concern over long periods of operation. When checking starter troubles, first ensure that the battery is in good condition and that all battery and starter connections are in good order. A corroded battery terminal or bad earth connection may have sufficient electrical resistance to make the starter inoperative, though enough current may be available for lamps and accessories. The details given in **FIG 11:14** will guide dismantling and reassembly if required, but if trouble is

experienced it is advised that the motor should be renewed on an exchange basis through an accredited service agent.

11:10 Headlamp dismantling, beam setting

On Ami 6 and 8 saloons the headlamp bulbs can be renewed without having to take out the beam units. Open the bonnet and swing out the bulb retaining clips with the fingers, when the bulb can be pulled out and detached from the leads connector. The new bulb can then be inserted and clipped into place.

On Dyane saloons either Cibie or SEV headlamps may be fitted. The embellishment collar on the former is pulled out towards the front, when the lamp assembly can be withdrawn by pressing on the spring 1 (see **FIG 11 : 15**) to release the tongue 2. The adjusting screws V should not be altered. On the SEV type (see **FIG 11 : 16**), similarly remove the embellisher and withdraw the assembly by the buckle 1 after removing the retaining screw. To renew a bulb (see **FIG 11 : 17**) disconnect the connector A and open the springs C and D securing the bulb collar. Fit the new bulb and refit the springs and connector. When refitting the embellisher ensure that the internal clips engage in the springs provided.

The 2CV has a single screw on top of the headlamp which must be removed to release the light unit when changing a bulb.

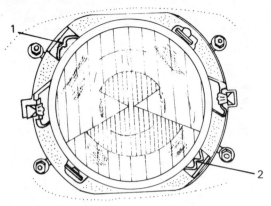

FIG 11:19 Headlamp adjusting screws 1 and 2

Initial adjustment of the headlamps is necessary, notwithstanding that a manual control under the instrument panel allows for height adjustment to suit the load whilst the vehicle is being driven. The makers recommend that the normal adjustment of the headlamps should be made by a proprietary Reglolux or Regloscope unit. If such a unit is not available the apparatus shown in FIG 11:18 is used in service.

Preliminary operations are to ensure that the tyre pressures are correct, the underbody heights (see Chapter 8) properly adjusted, the vehicle located on a flat horizontal surface and with loading of the tool kit, spare wheel and 5 litre of fuel in the tank. The control button is fully adjusted anticlockwise to the end of its travel. Any flat surface may be similarly employed with less accuracy, but with the special apparatus the flexible cables C are stretched with equal tension to the towing connections on the car. The vertical cords on the screen are located the same distance apart as the centres of the headlamps, with the horizontal cord situated at the height of the headlamp centres from the ground. The general procedure is then to use the adjusting screw 1 (see FIG 11:19) to line up the dipped beams on the horizontal cord B. Then with the main beams switched on, unscrew the manual control to centre the beams on the cord B. Proceed to use the adjusting screw 2 to centre the beams at the intersections 0 of the cords A and B.

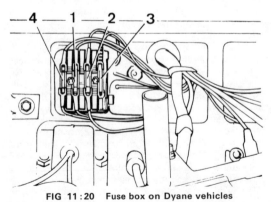

FIG 11:20 Fuse box on Dyane vehicles

Key to colour coding 1 Red 2 Blue 3 Yellow 4 Green

11:11 Fuses

As shown in the wiring diagrams all wires connected to the fuses are colour coded for identification. One 16 amp and two 10 amp fuses are provided in early Ami vehicles with an additional 16 amp spare fuse in later models. Four 16 amp fuses are fitted in Dyane cars as shown in FIG 11:20 up to 1970, when three fuses were provided. The fuse boxes are fitted to the rear of the dash panel under the bonnet. Before renewing a faulty fuse it is important to investigate the cause of failure otherwise it will probably recur. Reference to the wiring diagrams will assist in tracing faults.

The coding colours protect the following circuits:

1 Red	Front and rear lights, instrument panel and rear number plate.	
2 Blue	Wiper motor, fuel gauge, direction indicators, alternator field.	
3 Yellow	Stop lights, parking lights, interior lights	
4 Green	Spare or heater motor if fitted.	

11:12 Windscreen wipers

The procedure for removing the windscreen wiper assembly varies according to model type and year. The following details are typical and the relevant items may be applied to most models.

Removal:

Disconnect the battery and remove the wiper arms by folding them forwards and pulling them off their splined spindles.

Unscrew the securing nuts for the spindle bushings and remove the washers and rubber seals.

Remove the two press buttons and lift away the side trim panel.

Remove the upper part of the facia panel as follows: Take out the retaining screw and unclip the shock absorbing strip, then remove seven retaining screws, two at the front, three at the righthand side and two on the left. Lift off the upper panel.

Next remove the central section of the facia panel which is retained by a screw at the back of the parcel tray, a bolt at the bottom of the tray and a screw behind the steering wheel. The panel will now come away with the heater controls.

Remove the driver's side air vent.

Detach the two wiper spindle bushings.

Disconnect the wires to the wiper motor and supply cable to the accessory terminal on the shelf.

Remove the wiper assembly support by removing the upper bolt and the two lower screws and disconnecting the earth wire(s).

Detach the wiring from the support bracket and the locating plate from the upper mounting and remove the wiper assembly together with its support.

Refitting:

This is a reversal of the removal procedure, but note the position of the three wires to the motor. Black to the terminal +, blue to terminal IN and white to terminal AR. The black wire with the spade connector goes on the accessory terminal.

Lubricate the spindles with Caltex anti-rust oil or grease, together with other moving parts.

Adjust the position of the wiper arms on the splined spindles so that the blades are 50 + 5 mm above the bottom edge of the windscreen.

11:13 Fault diagnosis

(a) Battery discharged

1 Terminals or earth connection loose or dirty
2 Lighting circuit shorted
3 Alternator not charging
4 Regulator defective
5 Battery internally defective

(b) Insufficient charging current

1 Loose or corroded battery terminals
2 Alternator driving belt slipping

(c) Battery will not hold charge

1 Low electrolyte level
2 Battery plates sulphated
3 Electrolyte leaking from casing or top sealing compound
4 Separators ineffective

(d) Starter motor lacks power or will not operate

1 Battery discharged
2 Loose connections on battery or starter
3 Faulty earth connection
4 Starter pinion jammed in mesh with flywheel gear
5 Solenoid switch faulty
6 Brushes worn or sticking, leads detached or shorting
7 Commutator worn, burnt or shorted
8 Starter shaft bent
9 Engine abnormally stiff

(e) Starter motor runs but does not turn engine

1 Broken teeth on pinion or flywheel gear
2 Engagement mechanism faulty

(f) Noisy starter pinion when engine is running

1 Control spring weak or broken

(g) Starter motor inoperative

1 Check 1 and 6 in (d)
2 Armature or field coils faulty

(h) Starter motor rough or noisy

1 Mounting bolts loose
2 Damaged pinion or flywheel ring gear
3 Main pinion spring broken

(j) Lamps inoperative or erratic

1 Battery low, bulbs burned out
2 Faulty earthing of lamps or battery
3 Lighting switch faulty
4 Loose or broken wiring connections

(k) Wiper motor sluggish, taking high current

1 Faulty armature
2 Bearings out of alignment
3 Commutator dirty or short-circuited

(l) Fuel gauge does not register

1 No battery supply to gauge
2 Gauge casing not earthed
3 Cable between gauge and tank unit earthed

NOTES

CHAPTER 12

THE BODYWORK

12:1 Introduction

A welded sheet steel floor panel forms the basis on which the main components of the body shell are mounted. Most elements are of welded construction, but detachable parts of the superstructure consist of the bonnet, the front and rear wings, the wing arches, the front and rear doors and the tailgate door where provided.

2CV and Dyane vehicles are provided with a canvas roof which can be opened to two positions. Once wet, the hood should not be allowed to dry when rolled up. The rear seat can be readily removed to enable large loads to be carried.

Large-scale repairs to body panels and wings are best left to the expert panel beaters. Even small dents can be tricky, as too much hammering will stretch the metal and make things worse instead of better. Filling minor dents and scratches is probably the best method of restoring the surface. Use a modern filling compound and work to the manufacturer's instructions. The touching-up of paintwork is well within the ability of most owners, particularly as self-spraying cans of the correct colours are usually available. Paint may change colour with age and it is better to spray a whole wing or panel rather than to touch up a small area.

Before spraying, remove all traces of wax polish with white spirit. More drastic treatment will be required if silicone polish has been applied. Use a primer surfacer or a paste stopper or a filler according to the amount of filling required, and when it is dry, rub it down with 400 grade 'wet or dry' paper until the surface is smooth and flush with the surrounding area. Spend time on getting a good finish as this will control the final effect. Apply the retouching paint, keeping it wet in the centre and light round the edges. After a few hours drying, use a cutting compound to remove the dry spray. At this stage it will be evident whether the whole wing or panel should be sprayed. Finish off with a liquid polish.

12:2 Removing door trim

To remove the door trim or inner panel the armrest must be removed to obtain access to the panel retaining nuts. Insert a rule or other metal strip between the trim and the armrest to assist in the disengagement of the fasteners, then pull the armrest to the rear and upwards to remove it. Remove the two nuts and washers and take off the trim by levering with a thin screwdriver blade to disengage the securing clips.

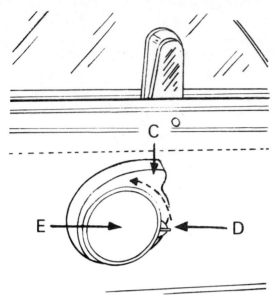

FIG 12:1   Door lock control, Ami 8

Key to Fig 12:1   **C** Lever   **D** Lever   **E** Pressbutton

12:3 Servicing door locks, remote control gear

To open a door from the inside on Ami 8 saloons, the handle is gripped and the release catch pulled back with the thumb. To lock the rear doors and the front lefthand door, the catch is pushed forward. A plunger is pressed down to unlock the doors. The front righthand door is locked with the ignition key. On Ami 8 cars the knob C (see **FIG 12:1**) is turned towards the rear to open the door. The latch D is pressed downwards to lock the door and unlocking is effected by pressing on the centre disc E. On AK vans the front righthand door is locked with the ignition key, as are the rear doors. The front lefthand door is locked by pressing down the small lever on the lock.

The locking mechanism on Dyane 4 vehicles is shown in **FIG 12:2**. On later Dyane vehicles a sliding lever is provided for opening doors from the inside and a catch for locking the door.

To remove a door lock and interior control on Ami vehicles, remove the door trim as previously described. Proceed to remove the locking button by turning it to the bottom, pressing on the side of the button and inserting a thin blade under the button on the opposite side. The button may then be levered up to disengage it. Detach the control rod and remove the lock fixing screws. Remove the external fittings and then remove the lock. Refit in the reverse order of the removal operations.

Details of the locks and the lock controls on Dyane 4 vehicles are shown in **FIG 12:2**. Removal operations are as follows:

1 Remove the trim panel as described in the previous Section.
2 Remove the pushbutton 6 from its housing 5. The pushbuttons are designed for a minimum pressure of 20 kg and if the button is loose on removal the housing 5 should be renewed.
3 To remove the barrel 7, press it out through the hole 'a' shown in **FIG 12:3**.
4 Disconnect the bearing 1 (see **FIG 12:4**) from the control rod 2.
5 Remove the three screws 4 (see **FIG 12:5**) securing the lock, the control rod 2, and the nuts 12 (see **FIG 12:6**) retaining the outside handle. Withdraw the lock, including the handle fitting 10, the guide 13, the pushbutton and the closing plate 9.
6 Refit in the reverse order of the removal operations. Note that the three screws 4 are tightened to a torque of 3 kg m, and that the hole 'a' of the pushbutton with locking device must be positioned to the front of the vehicle.

12:4 Window removal and refitting

Removal of door windows is undertaken as follows:
1 Slide both windows towards the front of the door.
2 Using a screwdriver disengage the slide 1 (see **FIG**

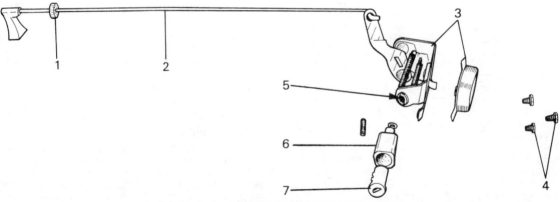

FIG 12:2   An exploded view of a door lock control

Key to Fig 12:2   1 Bearing   2 Control rod   3 Lock and external cover   4 Screws   5 Pushbutton housing   6 Pushbutton body   7 Barrel

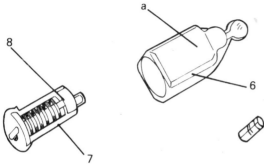

FIG 12:3 Pushbutton details

Key to Fig 12:3   6 Body   7 Barrel   8 Spring

12:7) from the rear vertical channel. The window guides are secured by clips.

3 Raise the rear section 2 from the lower channel.

4 Disengage from the rear and remove the plastic support 3. Replace the lower glass slide on the door.

5 Position the two glasses in the middle of the lower channel, then disengage the front glass by bearing on the lower channel so that the glass clears the upper channel.

6 Refitting is undertaken in the reverse manner of disassembly. Note that the correct fitting of the plastic support 3 is made with the notch on the lower edge towards the outside of the door. Push the support towards the front, under the lower slide 2, when it should fit in the position in the door provided for the purpose.

Remove the glass and its rubber seal (see **FIG 12:8**) from a quarter window, release the sealing surround by pressing on the interior of the glass towards the outside at the top of the glass at 'a'. The glass and its seal may then together be removed.

To fit a new glass and its seal, place a cord of about 4 mm diameter in the rubber surround together with the glass, crossing the ends of the cord at the centre of the bottom of the glass. Place the assembly in the body frame with the ends of the cord inside. Pull on the cord (see **FIG 12:9**) whilst an assistant taps on the glass from the outside with a soft mallet, so that the glass and surround fit into place as the operation proceeds.

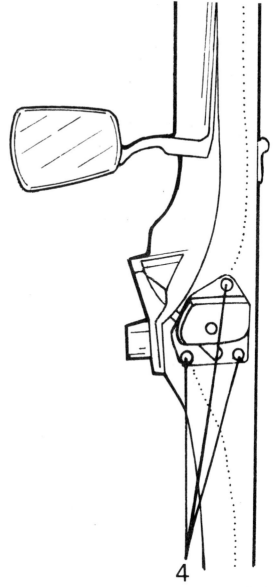

FIG 12:5   Showing the door lock fixing screws 4

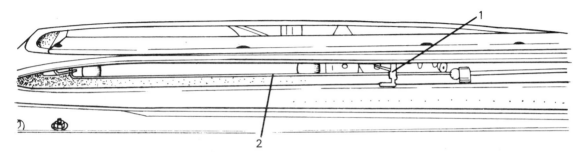

FIG 12:4   Location of control rod 2 and bearing 1

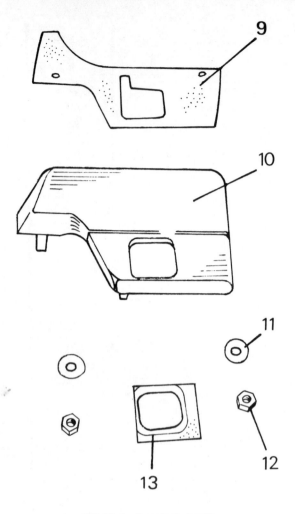

FIG 12:6   Door lock details

Key to Fig 12:6   9 Closing plate   10 Handle fitting
11 Washers   12 Nuts   13 Guide

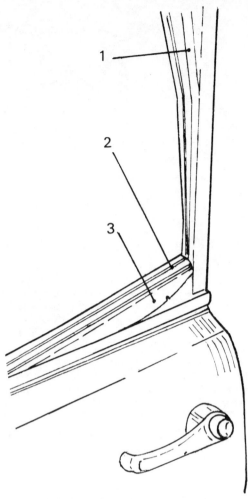

FIG 12:7   Removing door windows

Key to Fig 12:7   1 Vertical slide   2 Lower slide
3 Support

Winding windows:

To remove a window glass, it is necessary first to remove the armrest from the door and then the winding handle. This is done by pressing in the bezel and pushing out the retaining pin which will be seen underneath.

Lever off the door trim panel and remove the two plastic weathersheets and the spring on the winding shaft.

Refer to **FIG 12:10** and remove the four screws 1 securing the window regulating mechanism 2. Push the mechanism towards the rear of the door in order to disengage the rollers from the two glass carriers 3 and 4 and withdraw the mechanism from the door.

Swing the glass towards the front to free it from the vertical channel and lift it out of the door on the outside.

Refitting is the reverse of the removal procedure, after which any adjustment necessary can be made. This is simply a matter of positioning the winding mechanism

and the lower vertical channel 5 in the mounting screw holes so that a smooth and correct movement of the glass is obtained. Tighten the securing screws when satisfactory.

12:5 Front and rear wings

The following operations refer to Dyane 4 vehicles but will serve as a general guide for other models. To remove and refit a front wing, proceed as follows:
1 Referring to **FIGS 12:11** and **12:12**, disconnect the wiring loom 1 and the headlamp connector 3.
2 Remove the seven screws 4 retaining the wing on the wheel arch. Remove the retaining clip 5 of the mudshield and the screw 6.
3 Remove the two screws 3 (see **FIG 12:13**) holding the wing on the body structure. Remove the screw 4 holding the support on the floor panel and withdraw the wing.

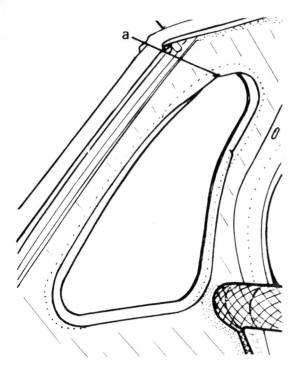

FIG 12:8 Quarter window, showing pressure point for removal at a

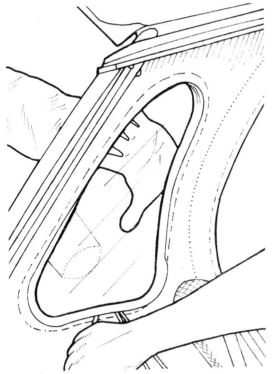

FIG 12:9 Fitting a quarter window showing the crossed ends of the cord at the bottom centre

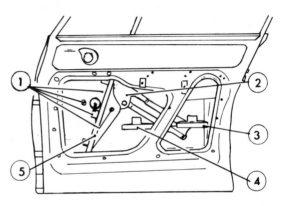

FIG 12:10 Removing the door window regulating mechanism

Key to Fig 12:10   1 Regulator securing screws
2 Regulator   3 Glass carrier   4 Glass carrier   5 Vertical channel

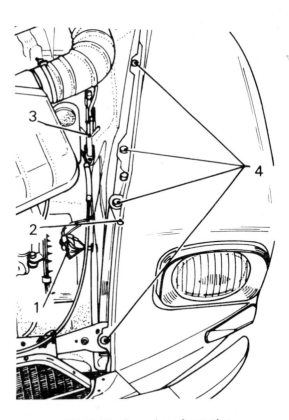

FIG 12:11   Removing a front wing

Key to Fig 12:11   1 Wiring assembly   2 Location point
3 Headlamp connection   4 Screws

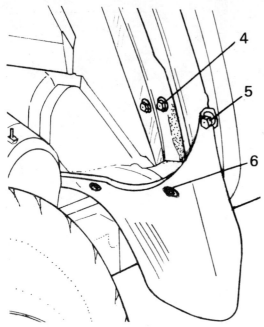

FIG 12:12 Removing a front wing, showing the screws 4 and 6 and the clip 5

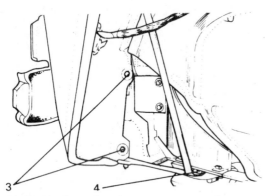

FIG 12:13 Removing a front wing, showing the screws 3 and 4

4 Commence refitting by locating the wing as at 2 in **FIG 12:11** and inserting without tightening the screws indicated.

5 Adjust the position of the wing in relation to the body by the screws 3 (see **FIG 12:13**). An even setting should be obtained between the wing flange and the front door, the wing flange and the bonnet and between the wing and the bonnet at the front. Finally tighten all the securing screws.

In the case of a rear wing, remove the securing screws shown in **FIGS 12:14, 12:15** and **12:16** and withdraw the wing. Refitting is simply the reverse procedure, ensuring that the sealing strip 3 is correctly positioned. Tighten the three screws 2 and the five screws 4 to a torque of .6 kg m.

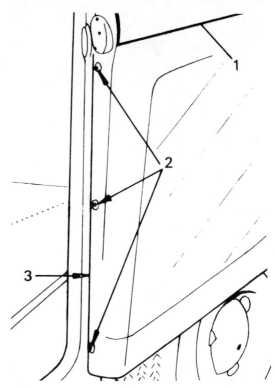

FIG 12:14 Removing a rear wing, showing the embellishment 1, the screws 2 and the sealing strip 3

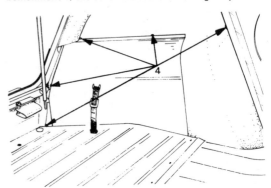

FIG 12:15 Removing a rear wing, showing the five screws 4

12:6 Seats

In Ami 6 saloons the forward adjustment of the front bench seat is 15 cm and controlled by lifting the handle provided. To take out the seat, pull the latch 1 (see **FIG 12:17**) backwards and upwards and then tilt the seat to the front to release the two front locating studs. Relatch the seat after refitting.

To take out the rear bench seat, first unlatch it by turning the latch at the rear and at the bottom of the centre part of the seat frame. Then tilt the seat forward to free it from its locating studs.

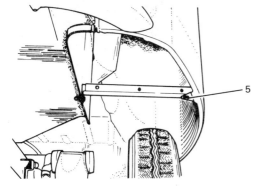

FIG 12:16   Removing a rear wing, showing the screw 5

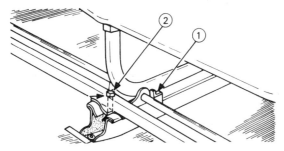

FIG 12:17   Adjusting a front bench seat on Ami 6 cars, showing the locking devices at 1 and 2

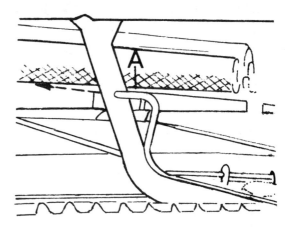

FIG 12:18   Adjusting a front bench seat on Ami 8 cars, showing the lever A

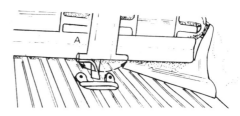

FIG 12:19   Adjustment of rear seat on Ami 8 cars, showing the rotation of the lever A

In Ami 8 saloons the front bench seat is adjusted by pushing the lever under the seat frame centre to the right. The seat is removed by taking out the retaining pin and pushing the seat as far back as it will go, whilst holding the lever A (see **FIG 12:18**) upwards to free the seat from its three slides. Reinsert the retaining pin on refitting.

The rear bench seat is unlatched for removal by swinging the handle A (see **FIG 12:19**) through 180 deg. and tilting the seat forwards to release it from its locating stud.

In AK-B vans the front seat is secured to the floor by a latch on the inside of the seat frame. To move the seat, turn the latch key so that the retaining pin is opposite its release aperture. Relatch the seat after its required adjustment. On other models procedure is similar except for different designs of securing devices.

12:7 Heating and ventilation

A very simple system of piping is used to convey hot air from two heat exchangers in the engine compartment and various methods of controlling the temperature and directing the air flow are used, a typical layout being shown in **FIG 12:20**. In this layout of the controls the vertical lever directs the airflow up to the windscreen or down to the under panel area, while the horizontal control regulates the amount of heating applied as the lever is moved from one side to another.

For ventilation the amount and direction of fresh air flowing through the grilles at each end of the instrument panel can be adjusted by the two levers provided. Moving the levers away from each other varies the amount of air

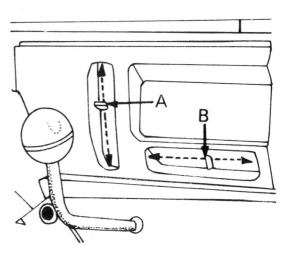

FIG 12:20   Heater control levers A and B on Ami 8 cars

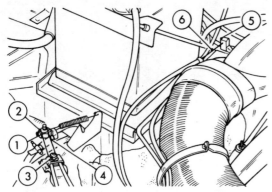

FIG 12:21   Adjusting the heating and ventilation control cables

Key to Fig 12:21   1 Heater cable securing screw   2 Clamp   3 Nut   4 Screw   5 Demist cable securing screw   6 Demist cable

supplied and moving them in the same direction adjusts the direction of the air flow. Deflectors are fitted on the scuttle in Ami 6 cars. With both levers lying alongside each other the air flow is cut off. Ventilation is also provided by the door sliding windows after releasing the latches and moving them to the position desired.

There is very little to go wrong with these systems, the only moving parts being the control linkages. With long use, however, it may become necessary to adjust the control cables to ensure correct operation, this can be carried out as follows:

Adjusting the heat regulator (see FIG 12:21):

Move the horizontal control lever on the panel fully to the left and loosen the screw 1 which retains the control cable to the clamp 2.

Push both lefthand and righthand levers operating the two heating valves towards the outside of the car so that they completely close the two air outlets.

Pull the cable sheath back about 20 mm to avoid bending the cable, then secure the nut 3 on the righthand heat exchanger clamp and the cable securing screws 1 and 4 on the clamp 9.

Adjusting the de-mist control:

Move the vertical lever on the instrument panel fully upwards.

Unscrew the screw 5 securing the end of the control cable 6 on the operating lever, then pull the lever towards the front and secure the screw 5.

After carrying out any adjustment on these cables, always operate them a few times from one stop to the other to check for correct operation.

APPENDIX

TECHNICAL DATA

HINTS ON MAINTENANCE AND OVERHAUL

GLOSSARY OF TERMS

Inches	Decimals	Milli-metres	Inches to Millimetres		Millimetres to Inches	
			Inches	mm	mm	Inches
1/64	.015625	.3969	.001	.0254	.01	.00039
1/32	.03125	.7937	.002	.0508	.02	.00079
3/64	.046875	1.1906	.003	.0762	.03	.00118
1/16	.0625	1.5875	.004	.1016	.04	.00157
5/64	.078125	1.9844	.005	.1270	.05	.00197
3/32	.09375	2.3812	.006	.1524	.06	.00236
7/64	.109375	2.7781	.007	.1778	.07	.00276
1/8	.125	3.1750	.008	.2032	.08	.00315
9/64	.140625	3.5719	.009	.2286	.09	.00354
5/32	.15625	3.9687	.01	.254	.1	.00394
11/64	.171875	4.3656	.02	.508	.2	.00787
3/16	.1875	4.7625	.03	.762	.3	.01181
13/64	.203125	5·1594	.04	1.016	.4	.01575
7/32	.21875	5.5562	.05	1.270	.5	.01969
15/64	.234375	5.9531	.06	1.524	.6	.02362
1/4	.25	6.3500	.07	1.778	.7	.02756
17/64	.265625	6.7469	.08	2.032	.8	.03150
9/32	.28125	7.1437	.09	2.286	.9	.03543
19/64	.296875	7.5406	.1	2.54	1	.03937
5/16	.3125	7.9375	.2	5.08	2	.07874
21/64	.328125	8.3344	.3	7.62	3	.11811
11/32	.34375	8.7312	.4	10.16	4	.15748
23/64	.359375	9.1281	.5	12.70	5	.19685
3/8	.375	9.5250	.6	15.24	6	.23622
25/64	.390625	9.9219	.7	17.78	7	.27559
13/32	.40625	10.3187	.8	20.32	8	.31496
27/64	.421875	10.7156	.9	22.86	9	.35433
7/16	.4375	11.1125	1	25.4	10	.39370
29/64	.453125	11.5094	2	50.8	11	.43307
15/32	.46875	11.9062	3	76.2	12	.47244
31/64	.484375	12.3031	4	101.6	13	.51181
1/2	.5	12.7000	5	127.0	14	.55118
33/64	.515625	13.0969	6	152.4	15	.59055
17/32	.53125	13.4937	7	177.8	16	.62992
35/64	.546875	13.8906	8	203.2	17	.66929
9/16	.5625	14.2875	9	228.6	18	.70866
37/64	.578125	14.6844	10	254.0	19	.74803
19/32	.59375	15.0812	11	279.4	20	.78740
39/64	.609375	15.4781	12	304.8	21	.82677
5/8	.625	15.8750	13	330.2	22	.86614
41/64	.640625	16.2719	14	355.6	23	.90551
21/32	.65625	16.6687	15	381.0	24	.94488
43/64	.671875	17.0656	16	406.4	25	.98425
11/16	.6875	17.4625	17	431.8	26	1.02362
45/64	.703125	17.8594	18	457.2	27	1.06299
23/32	.71875	18.2562	19	482.6	28	1.10236
47/64	.734375	18.6531	20	508.0	29	1.14173
3/4	.75	19.0500	21	533.4	30	1.18110
49/64	.765625	19.4469	22	558.8	31	1.22047
25/32	.78125	19.8437	23	584.2	32	1.25984
51/64	.796875	20.2406	24	609.6	33	1.29921
13/16	.8125	20.6375	25	635.0	34	1.33858
53/64	.828125	21.0344	26	660.4	35	1.37795
27/32	.84375	21.4312	27	685.8	36	1.41732
55/64	.859375	21.8281	28	711.2	37	1.4567
7/8	.875	22.2250	29	736.6	38	1.4961
57/64	.890625	22.6219	30	762.0	39	1.5354
29/32	.90625	23.0187	31	787.4	40	1.5748
59/64	.921875	23.4156	32	812.8	41	1.6142
15/16	.9375	23.8125	33	838.2	42	1.6535
61/64	.953125	24.2094	34	863.6	43	1.6929
31/32	.96875	24.6062	35	889.0	44	1.7323
63/64	.984375	25.0031	36	914.4	45	1.7717

UNITS	Pints to Litres	Gallons to Litres	Litres to Pints	Litres to Gallons	Miles to Kilometres	Kilometres to Miles	Lbs. per sq. In. to Kg. per sq. Cm.	Kg. per sq. Cm. to Lbs. per sq. In.
1	.57	4.55	1.76	.22	1.61	.62	.07	14.22
2	1.14	9.09	3.52	.44	3.22	1.24	.14	28.50
3	1.70	13.64	5.28	.66	4.83	1.86	.21	42.67
4	2.27	18.18	7.04	.88	6.44	2.49	.28	56.89
5	2.84	22.73	8.80	1.10	8.05	3.11	.35	71.12
6	3.41	27.28	10.56	1.32	9.66	3.73	.42	85.34
7	3.98	31.82	12.32	1.54	11.27	4.35	.49	99.56
8	4.55	36.37	14.08	1.76	12.88	4.97	.56	113.79
9		40.91	15.84	1.98	14.48	5.59	.63	128.00
10		45.46	17.60	2.20	16.09	6.21	.70	142.23
20				4.40	32.19	12.43	1.41	284.47
30				6.60	48.28	18.64	2.11	426.70
40				8.80	64.37	24.85		
50					80.47	31.07		
60					96.56	37.28		
70					112.65	43.50		
80					128.75	49.71		
90					144.84	55.92		
100					160.93	62.14		

UNITS	Lb ft to kgm	Kgm to lb ft	UNITS	Lb ft to kgm	Kgm to lb ft
1	.138	7.233	7	.967	50.631
2	.276	14.466	8	1.106	57.864
3	.414	21.699	9	1.244	65.097
4	.553	28.932	10	1.382	72.330
5	.691	36.165	20	2.765	144.660
6	.829	43.398	30	4.147	216.990

TECHNICAL DATA

Dimensions are in mm unless otherwise stated

ENGINE DETAILS

Cubic capacity:
Types A53 and A79/0	425 cc
Type A79/1	435 cc
Types M4, M28 and M28/1	602 cc

Bore and stroke:
425 cc	66 × 62
435 cc	68.5 × 59
602 cc	74 × 70

Compression ratio:
Type A53	7.5 : 1
Types A79/0 and M4	7.75/1
Types A79/1 and M28/1	8.5 : 1
Type M28	9 : 1

Camshaft:
Material	Cast iron
Drive	Gear
Number of bearings	2
Bearing diameters	Front 36 Rear 20
Thrust	Carried on front bearing
End float	.04 to .09

Connecting rods:
Type	Steel forgings, integral with bearing shells on crankshaft and not dismantlable
End float	.08 to .13
Small end bush inside diameter	20.000 to 20.016

Crankshaft:
Type	Steel forging assembly of five parts shrink fitted with two main bearings and two crankpins
Nominal journal diameter	Front 48 Rear 52
Dyane 4	Front 43 Rear 48
Nominal crankpin diameter	39
Dyane 4	38
End float	.07 to .14

Bearing shells:
Diametrical clearance	.055 to .111

(Note: The front shell is retained behind the crankshaft pinion and is supplied
assembled with the crankshaft, as are the connecting rods)

Engine lubrication:
Lubrication system	Pressure feed

Oil pressure:
Engines A79/1	57 to 71 lb/sq inch at 6000 rev/min
Engines M28/1, M28	78 to 92 lb/sq inch at 6000 rev/min
Engines A53, A79/0, M4	35 to 44 lb/sq inch at 4000 rev/min
Oil pump	Gear type. Backlash between teeth is set in manufacture and is not adjustable
Filtration	Sump strainer or external oil filter

Sump capacity (litre):

	After draining	After removing rocker cover
A53	2.0	2.2
A79/0—A79/1	2.0	2.3
M4	2.5	2.85
M28/1—M28	2.2	2.5
Oil cooler capacity	105 cc	
Difference between minimum and maximum on dipstick	.5 litre	

Pistons:

Material	Light alloy
Number of piston rings	1 compression, 1 scraper, 1 oil control

Ring gap:

Compression ring	.20 to .35	.30 to .45
Scraper ring	.10 to .25	.25 to .40
Oil control ring	.15 to .30	.20 to .35
Clearance in cylinder bore	.05 to .07	

Note: Replacement pistons, rings and gudgeon pins are not available

Valves:

	Inlet	Exhaust
Seat angle	120°	90°
Head diameter:		
A53—A79/0	39	32
A79/1—M4	39	34
M28/1—M28	40	34
Stem diameter	8	8.5
Clearances (cold)	0.20	0.20

Valve springs:

	Outer	Inner
Length under load:		
A53, A79/0, M4	24 (48 kg)	15 (9.5 kg)
A79/1, M28/1, M28	31 (28 kg)	24 (12 kg)

Valve timing:

Engine type	A53, M4	A79/0	A79/1	M28/1, M28
Inlet opens BTDC ...	3°	12°	2° 5'	0° 5'
Inlet closes ABDC ...	45°	54°	41° 30'	49° 15'
Exhaust opens BBDC ...	45°	55°	35° 55'	35° 55'
Exhaust closes ATDC ...	11°	21°	3° 30'	3° 30'

FUEL SYSTEM

Carburetter details:

Solex 26/35:	May to November, 1968		November 1968 onwards	
	1st barrel	2nd barrel	1st barrel	2nd barrel
Diffuser	21	24	21	24
Main jet	120	60	125	70*
Compensating jet ...	1F1 (145)	2HI (145)	1F1 (145)	2AA (120)
Slow-running jet	50		50	
Pump jet	40		40	
Econostat	70		None	
Needle valve seat ...	1.7		1.7	
Float weight	5.7 g (double)		5.7 g (double)	

*75 with M28 engine since July 1969

Solex 34 PICS.4:	602 cc	435 cc
Diffuser	28	28
Main jet	160	155
Compensating jet	AB	AB
Slow-running jet	42.5	40
Pump jet	40	35
Needle valve seat	1.3	1.3
Float weight	5.7 g	5.7 g

Solex 34 PCIS-6 (Dyane):

Diffuser	28
Main jet	155
Compensating jet	AB
Bypass jet	50
Pump jet	35
Slow-running jet	40

Solex 34 PICS-6 (Utility):

Diffuser	28
Main jet	165
Compensating jet	AC
Bypass jet	52.5
Pump jet	40
Slow-running jet	42.5

Solex 26/35 CSIC and 26/35 SCIC (EEC):

	Primary	Secondary
Diffuser	21	24
Main jet	125	82.5
Compensating jet	1F1	2AA
Slow-running jet	40	
Pump jet	40	
Idle speed	750 to 800 rev/min	
CO content	.8 to 1.6 per cent	
CO_2 content	9 to 12.5 per cent	

Solex 32:

Venturi bore	28
Main jet	150
Compensating jet	215
Slow-running jet	55
Slow-running air jet	160
Needle valve seat	1.3
Float weight	5.7 g

Solex 30 and 40:

	30 PICS	40 PCIS	40 PCIS.2
Diffuser	26	32	32
Main jet	140	165	170
Compensating jet	AB	AC	AC
Slow-running jet	47	55	50
Slow-running air jet	160	130	130
Pump jet		40	40
Needle valve seat	1.3	1.3	1.3
Gasket	1	1.5	1.5
Float weight	5.7 g	5.7 g	5.7 g

Idling speeds:

Conventional clutch, A53	600 to 650 rev/min
A79/0, A79/1	800 to 850 rev/min
M4 (AYA3)	700 to 800 rev/min
M4 (AK)	650 to 700 rev/min
M28/1, M28	760 to 800 rev/min
Centrifugal clutch	Clutch just contacting drum, then loosen screw one-eighth of a turn

Fuel pump:

Make and type	SEV or Guiot, mechanical

Fuel tank capacities:

Ami 6 and Dyane 6	25 litres	5.5 gallons
Ami 8	32 litres	6.8 gallons
Dyane 4 and 2CV	20 litres	4.4 gallons

IGNITION SYSTEM

Distributor:

Type	Citroen, with 2-lobe cam on end of camshaft behind the cooling fan. No rotary distributor cap assembly
Contact breaker points gap	.4±.05. Maximum difference between lobes .05
Dwell angle	144±2 deg. (from 1970, 109±3 deg.)
Capacitor capacity	.18 to .22 microfarad
Static advance...	8 deg. BTDC (M28, M28/1)
	12 deg. BTDC (other engines)

Sparking plugs:

Ami 8	AC 42 FF
	Marchal 34S
Ami 6	AC 43F
	Champion XL 85
2CV	AC 42 FF
	Champion XL 85
	Marchal 35
Dyane 4 and 6, Mehari (up to 1970)	AC 42 FF
	Champion L 87 Y
	Marchal 34S
Dyane 4 and 6, Mehari (from 1970)	AC 42 FF
	Bosch W 225TI
	Champion L 85
	Marchal 34S or 35
Gap	.6 to .7

COOLING SYSTEM

Type	Cylinder heads and cylinders air cooled by an eight- or nine-bladed nylon fan. Airflow from fan also cools an oil radiator.

CLUTCH

Type	Single dry plate with optional centrifugal clutch mechanism
Clutch pedal free travel	20 to 25
Clutch fork free travel	1 to 1.5

GEARBOX

Overall gear ratios:

	First	Second	Third	Fourth	Reverse	Including final drive ratio
Ami 6 ...	.0492	.0952	.1432	.2097	.0492	8/29
*Ami 8 ...	.0448	.0879	.1341	.1911	.0448	8/31 *
AK ...	.0455	.0882	.1435	.1943	.0455	8/29
AKB ...	.0426	.0835	.1341	.1816	.0426	8/31
Dyane 4 (AYA) ...	.0352	.0767	.1293	.1773	.0327	8/29
2CV4 and Dyane 4 (AYA2)	.0348	.0682	.1136	.1645	.0348	8/33
2CV6 and Dyane 6	.0465	.0912	.1357	.1842	.0465	8/33

* Also Dyane 6 after 1970

Lubrication:
Grade of lubricant ... ... SAE EP.80
Gearbox oil capacity ... ... .9 litre

SUSPENSION

Type	Independent suspension on all four wheels by tubular arms in line with the chassis, the rear arms trailing from their pivots. A common interacting spring unit connects each pair of arms on each side of the vehicle
Dampers	Inertia dampers at each wheel; or telescopic hydraulic dampers in later models

Geometry:
Front, Camber ... ... 1 deg. + 45 − 25 min.
Castor ... ... 15 deg. 25 min.
Alignment ... ... 0 to 3 mm toe-out
Rear, Camber ... ... 0 to 30 min.
Alignment ... ... 4 mm toe-in to 4 mm toe-out

STEERING

Type ... ... Rack and pinion, no pinion adjustment
Steering rack ... ... Incorporated in front axle crossmember
Turning radius ... ... 5.3 m

BRAKES

Type ... ... Hydraulically operated drum-type. Front disc brakes on later Ami and Dyane models

Drum internal diameter:	Front	Rear
Nominal diameter	220 (3CV), 200 (2CV)	180
Maximum refacing	2	2

Disc thickness 7
Disc diameter 244
Disc runout ... ... .2 maximum
Fluid type:
Drum brakes ... ... Lockheed 55
Disc brake system ... ... Green LHM fluid

ELECTRICAL EQUIPMENT

Battery ... ... 12-volt, 30amp/hr or 6-volt, 45/50 amp/hr
DC generator ... ... Ducellier or Paris-Rhone
Alternator ... ... Ducellier or Paris-Rhone
Starter motor ... ... Ducellier or Paris-Rhone
Commutator minimum diameter:
Ducellier 32
Paris-Rhone 34.5

TIGHTENING TORQUES

Brakes:	kg m	lb ft
Caliper bolts	4.5 to 5	32 to 36
Brake disc	4.5 to 5	32 to 36
Brake pipe union	6 to 8	43 to 58
Fluid reservoir	4.5 to 5	32 to 36
Front brake drums	5 to 6	36 to 43
Master cylinder	1	7

	kgf m	lbf ft
Clutch:		
Centrifugal clutch carrier ring	.9 to 1.4	7 to 10
Centrifugal clutch drum	3 to 3.1	22 to 23
Engine:		
Cylinder head nuts:		
Pre-tightening	1 to 1.2	7 to 9
Final tightening	2 to 2.3	15 to 17
Crankcase bolts:		
7 mm diameter	1.9	14
10 mm diameter	4.5	32
Fan pulley nut	4	29
Flywheel bolts	4.2	30
Manifolds	1.5	11
Oil cooler	1.4 to 1.9	10 to 14
Oil strainer	.5	3.5
Relief valve plug	4 to 4.5	29 to 32
Rocker cover	.5 to .7	3.5 to 5
Front axle:		
Crossmember	5	36
Hub ringnut	34.5 to 39	250 to 281
Inertia damper	6	44
Stub axle carrier lever	1.5 to 2	11 to 15
Gearbox and transmission:		
Differential shaft bearing lockring	6 to 7.5	43 to 54
Differential shaft bearing cap nut	14 to 16	100 to 116
Differential shaft front bearing nut	10 to 12	72 to 87
Transmission to hub	34 to 39	250 to 281
Transmission to drum (single ball joints) ...	5 to 6	36 to 43
Transmission to drum (double ball joints) ...	2.5	18
Rear axle:		
Crossmember	4 to 5	29 to 36
Damper:		
Saloon	3.5	25
Estate	8.5	62
Hub bearing locknut	26.5 to 29.5	190 to 212
Suspension arm castellated nut	3 to 3.5	22 to 25
Wheel nuts	5 to 6	36 to 43
Steering:		
Anti-roll bar	6	43
Ball joint nylstop nut	3 to 4	22 to 29
Pinion collar	1.9	14
Pinion nut	10 to 14	72 to 100
Track rod bearing nuts...	3 to 4	22 to 29
Track rod clamp nuts	1	7
Suspension:		
Suspension cylinder	18 to 22	130 to 158

VEHICLE IDENTIFICATION

Vehicle	Code and dates	Engine type	Car-buretter
2CV4	AZ (Series A & AM) before 2/70	A53	A
2CV4	AZ (Series A2) from 2/70	A79/1	D or E
2CV6	AZ (Series KA) from 2/70	M28/1	D or E
Dyane	AYA (Series A & AM) 8/67 to 3/68	A79/0	B
Dyane 4	AYA2 (Series A & AM) 3/68 to 2/70	A79/1	C or E
Dyane 6	AYA3 (Series A & AM) 1/68 to 10/68	M4	F
Dyane 6	AYB (Series A & AM) 10/68 to 2/70	M28/1	C or D
Dyane	AYA2 (Series A & AM) from 2/70	A79/1	D

Dyane 6	AY (Series CB) from 2/70	M28	H
Ami 6	AM 5/61 to 5/68	M4	G
Ami 6	AM2 5/68 to 3/69	M28	H
Ami 8	AM3 (Series JA) from 3/69	M28	H
Ami 6 Estate	AMB 9/64 to 5/68	M4	G
Ami 6 Estate	AMB2 5/68 to 3/69	M28	H
Ami 8 Estate	AM3 (Series JB) from 3/69	M28	H
2CV Van	AZU (Series A) before 2/72	A53 or A79/0	A or B
Citroen 250	AZU (Series A) 2/72 to 8/72	A79/0	B
Citroen 250	AZU (Series B) from 8/72	A79/1	E
3CV Van	AK (Series A) before 5/68	M4	G
3CV Van	AK (Series B) 5/68 to 8/70	M28/1	C or D
Citroen 400	AK (Series AK) from 8/70	M28/1	D or E
Mehari	AY (Series CA)	M28/1	C, D or E

Carburetter identification:

Clutch type						*Conventional*	*Centrifugal*
A	...	...	...	...	...	Solex 28 IBC *or* Zenith 28 IN	Solex 28 CBI *or* Zenith 28 IN4
B	...	...	...	...	...	Solex 32 PICS	Solex 32 PCIS
C	...	...	...	...	...	Solex 34 PICS 4	Solex 34 PCIS 4
D	...	...	...	...	...	Solex 34 PICS 5	Solex 34 PCIS 5
E	...	...	...	...	...	Solex 34 PICS 6	Solex 34 PCIS 6
F	...	...	...	...	...	Solex 40 PICS 3	Solex 40 PCIS 3
G	...	...	...	...	...	Solex 30 PICS	—
H	...	...	...	...	...	Solex 26/35 CSIC	Solex 26/35 SCIC

TYRES

Size:

All models ... ... 125 × 15 in. Michelin 'X' only

Pressures:

All 2 CV and Dyane models ... ... 20 lb/sq in. (1.4 kg/sq cm) front
26 lb/sq in. (1.8 kg/sq cm) rear

Ami models ... ... 26 lb/sq in. (1.8 kg/sq cm) front
26 lb/sq in. (1.8 kg/sq cm) rear

WEIGHTS AND DIMENSIONS

						2CV	*Dyane*	*Ami*
Wheelbase	...	...	...	...	...	2400	2400	2400
Front track	...	...	...	...	...	1260	2400	1260
Rear track	...	...	...	...	...	1260	1260	1220
Overall length	...	...	...	...	...	3830	3870	3991
Overall width	...	...	...	...	...	1480	1500	1524
Overall height (empty)	...	...	...	...	1600	1540	1494
Ground clearance (laden)		...	...	...	150	155	130

Weights in kg:						*Unladen*	*Laden*
AZ (A & AM) ...	...	...	...	...	...	535	870
AZ (A2)	...	...	...	...	...	560	895
AZ (KA)	...	...	...	...	...	560	895
AYA (A)	...	...	...	...	...	570	910
AYA (AM)	...	...	...	...	...	575	910
AYA2 (A & AM)	...	...	...	...	...	590	925
AYA3 (A)	...	...	...	...	...	585	925
AYB3 (AM)	...	...	...	...	...	590	925
AYB (A & AM)	...	...	...	...	...	600	930
AY (CB)	...	...	...	...	...	600	930
AM & AM2	...	...	...	...	...	640	960
AM3 (J)	...	...	...	...	...	725	1050

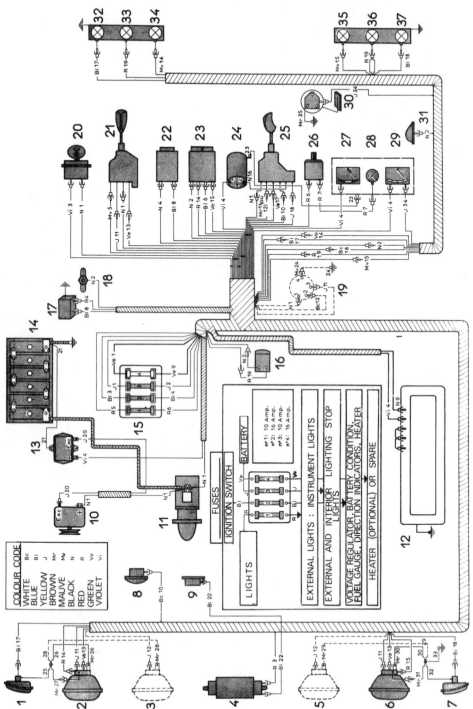

FIG 13:1   Wiring diagram Ami 6, from October, 1968

Key to Fig 13:1   1 Sidelight and direction indicator   2 Headlight   3 Auxiliary headlight   4 Ignition coil   5 Auxiliary headlight   6 Headlight   7 Sidelight and direction indicator   8 Horn   9 Distributor   10 Alternator   11 Starter   12 Heater (optional)   13 Lighting switch   14 Battery   15 Fuse box   16 Stoplight   17 Windscreen wiper motor   18 Accessory case   19 Auxiliary headlight relay   20 Ignition switch   21 Lighting switch   22 Windscreen wiper switch   23 Parking light switch   24 Flasher unit   25 Direction indicator, horn and headlight flasher switch   26 Instrument panel lighting rheostat   27 Thermal voltmeter   28 Instrument panel light   29 Fuel gauge   30 Fuel gauge tank unit   31 Interior light   32 Direction indicator   33 Stoplight   34 Rear light and number plate light   35 Rear light and number plate light   36 Stoplight   37 Direction indicator   Dotted lines apply to 'club' models

COLOUR CODE
WHITE — Bc
BLUE — Bl
YELLOW — J
BROWN — Mr
MAUVE — Mv
BLACK — N
RED — R
GREEN — Ve
VIOLET — Vi

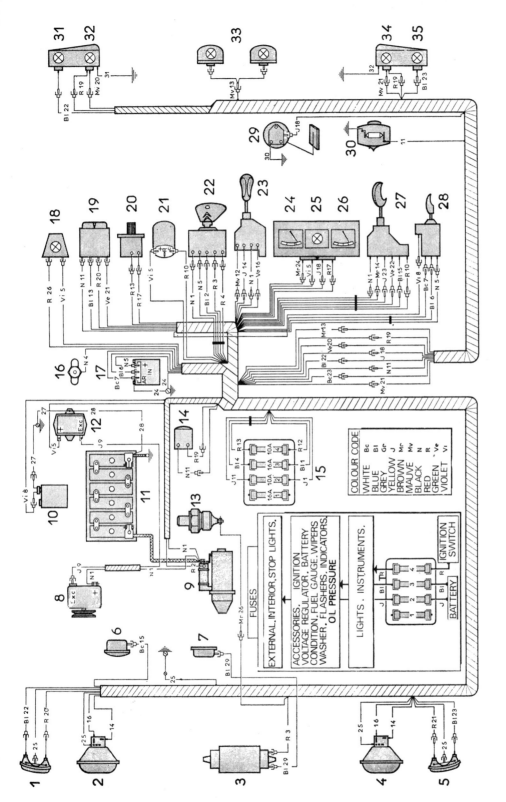

FIG 13:2 Wiring diagram Ami 8, from October, 1969. Similar for previous models except for items 13 and 18

Key to Fig 13:2 1 Sidelight and direction indicator 2 Headlight 3 Ignition coil 4 Headlight 5 Sidelight and direction indicator 6 Horn 7 Distributor 8 Alternator 9 Starter 10 Windscreen washer pump 11 Battery 12 Voltage regulator 13 Oil pressure switch 14 Stop switch 15 Fuse box 16 Accessory case 17 Windscreen wiper motor 18 Oil pressure warning light 19 Parking light switch 20 Instrument panel lighting rheostat 21 Flasher unit 22 Ignition, anti-theft and starter switch 23 Lighting switch 24 Thermal voltmeter 25 Instrument panel light 26 Fuel gauge 27 Direction indicator, headlight flasher and horn switch 28 Windscreen wiper and windscreen washer switch 29 Fuel gauge tank unit 30 Interior light 31 Direction indicator 32 Rear and stop light 33 Number plate light 34 Stoplight 35 Direction indicator

DYANE

127

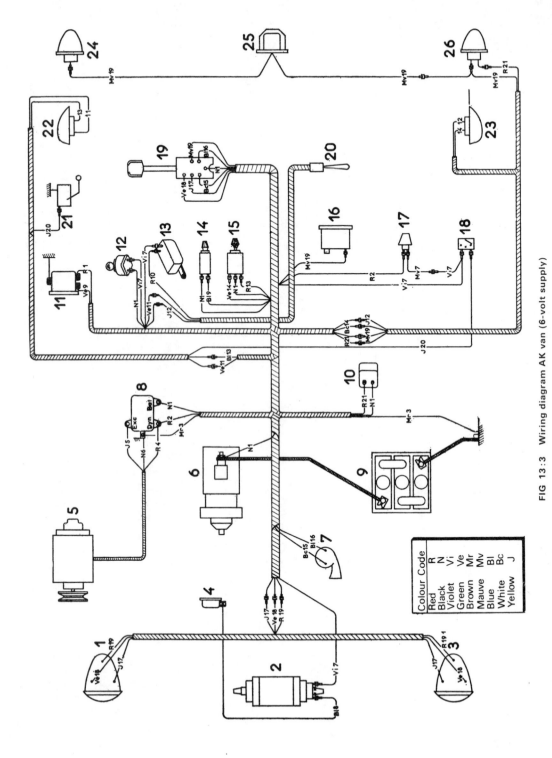

FIG 13:3 Wiring diagram AK van (6-volt supply)

Key to Fig 13:3 1 Headlight 2 Ignition coil 3 Headlight 4 Distributor 5 DC generator 6 Starter 7 Horn 8 Regulator 9 Battery 10 Stop switch 11 Wiper motor 12 Ignition switch 13 Direction indicators switch 14 Wiper switch 15 Sidelights switch 16 Speedometer 17 Charge indicator 18 Fuel gauge 19 Lighting and horn switch 20 Direction indicators switch 21 Fuel tank gauge 22/23 Sidelights and indicator switches 24/26 Rear lights 25 Number plate

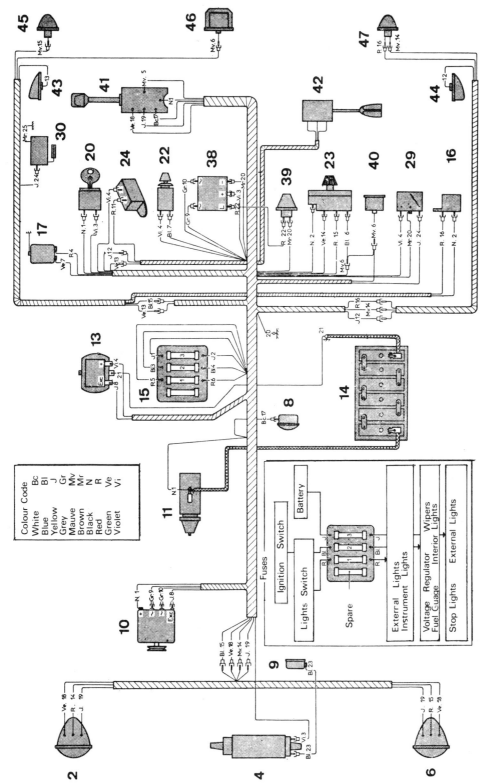

FIG 13 : 4   Wiring diagram, AK van (12-volt supply)

Colour Code
White   Bc
Blue   Bl
Yellow   J
Grey   Gr
Mauve   Mv
Brown   Mr
Black   N
Red   R
Green   Ve
Violet   Vi

Key to Fig 13:4   2 Headlight   **4** gnition coil   **6** Headlight   **8** Horn   **9** Distributor   **10** Alternator   **11** Starter   **13** Voltage regulator   **14** Battery   **15** Fuse box
16 Stoplight   **17** Windscreen wiper motor   **20** Ignition switch   **22** Windscreen wiper switch   **23** Parking light switch   **29** Flasher unit   **30** Fuel gauge
tank unit   **38** Charge-discharge warning light relay   **39** Charge-discharge warning light   **40** Speedometer   **41** Horn and lighting switch   **42** Direction indicator switch
43 Direction indicator   **44** Direction indicator   **45** Rear light   **46** Number plate   **47** Rear and stoplight

DYANE

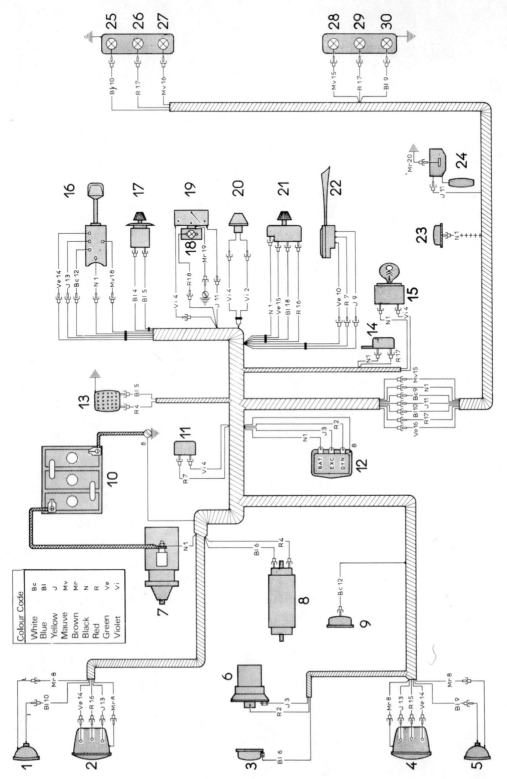

FIG 13:5 Wiring diagram Dyane 4 (6-volt supply)

Key to Fig 13:5 1/5 Direction indicators 2/4 Headlights 3 Distributor 6 DC generator 7 Starter 8 Ignition coil 9 Horn 10 Battery 11 Direction indicator switch box 12 Regulator 13 Wiper motor 14 Stop switch 15 Ignition switch 16 Lights and horn switch 17 Wiper switch 18 Instrument panel 19 Fuel gauge 20 Charge indicator 21 Sidelights switch 22 Direction indicators switch 23 Interior light 24 Fuel gauge 25/30 Direction indicators 26/29 Stop lights 27/28 Rear and number plate lights

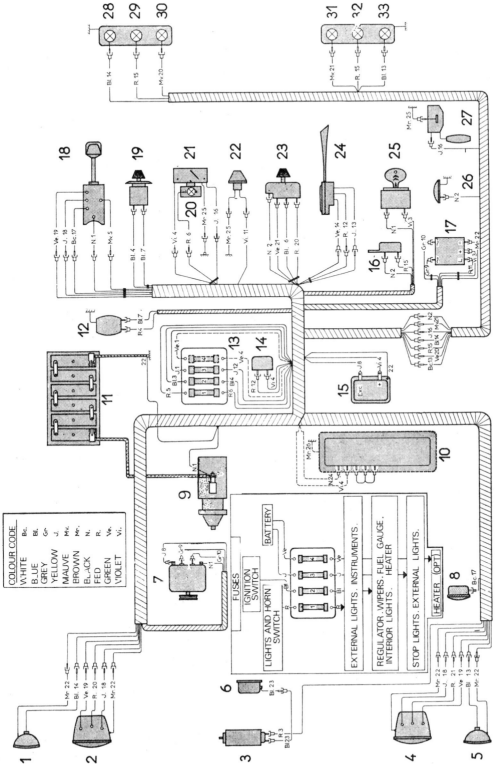

FIG 13:6   Wiring diagram Dyane 6 (12-volt supply)

COLOUR CODE

WHITE	Bc.
BLUE	Bl.
GREY	Gr
YELLOW	J.
MAUVE	Mv.
BROWN	Mr.
BLACK	N.
RED	R.
GREEN	Ve.
VIOLET	Vi.

Key to Fig 13:6 1/5 Direction indicators   2/4 Headlights   3 Ignition coil   6 Distributor   7 Alternator   8 Horn   9 Starter motor   10 Heater   11 Battery   12 Wiper motor   13 Fuses   14 Direction indicator control box   15 Regulator   16 Stop switch   17 Charge indicator relay   18 Lighting and horn switch   19 Wiper switch   20 Instrument panel   21 Fuel gauge   22 Charge indicator   23 Sidelights switch   24 Direction indicators switch   25 Ignition switch   26 Interior light   27 Fuel gauge   28/33 Direction indicators   29/32 Stop lights   30/31 Rear and number plate lights

DYANE

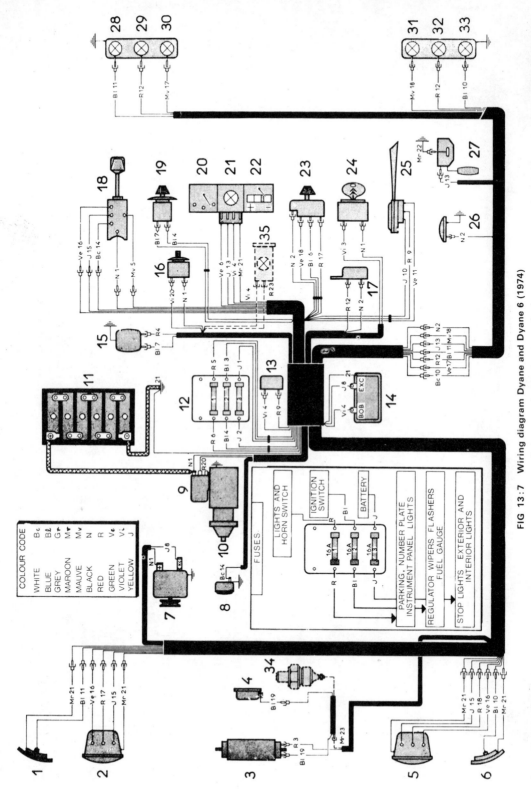

FIG 13:7 Wiring diagram Dyane and Dyane 6 (1974)

Key to Fig 13:7   1/6 Direction indicators   2/5 Headlamps   3 Coil   4 Distributor   7 Alternator   8 Horn   9 Solenoid   10 Starter motor   11 Battery   12 Fuse box
13 Flasher unit   14 Regulator   15 Windscreen wiper   16 Starter switch   17 Stop switch   18 Lights and horn switch   19 Wiper switch   20 Fuel gauge
21 Panel lamp   22 Battery condition indicator   23 Parking light indicator   24 Ignition switch   25 Flasher switch   26 Interior light   27 Fuel tank unit   28/33 Rear
direction indicators   29/32 Stop lamps   30/31 Rear and number plate lamps   34 Oil pressure switch   35 Oil pressure warning lamp

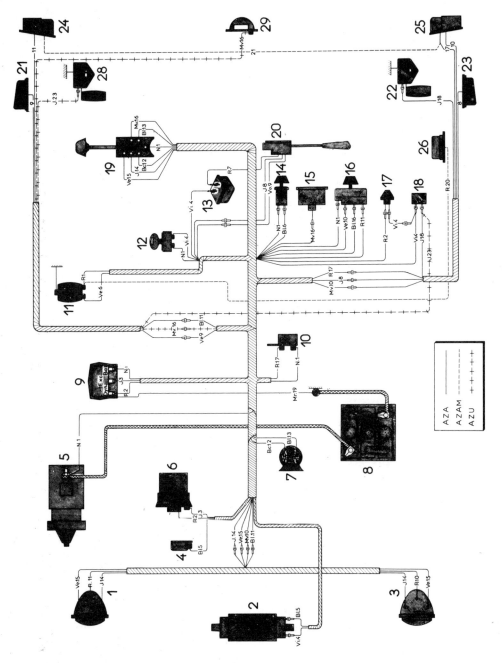

FIG 13:8   Wiring diagram 2CV4 and 6 (6-volt supply)

Key to Fig 13:8 1, 3 Headlamps 2 Coil 4 Distributor 5 Starter 6 Dynamo 7 Horn 8 Battery 9 Regulator 10 Stop lamp switch 11 Wiper motor 12 Ignition switch 13 Flasher unit 14 Wiper switch 15 Speedometer 16 Parking light switch 17 Charge indicator 18 Fuel gauge 19 Horn and lighting switch 20 Direction indicator switch 21, 23 Direction indicators 22 Fuel gauge rheostat 24, 25 Rear light units 26 Interior lamp 28 Fuel gauge rheostat (AZU) Number plate lamp (AZU)

Colour code: **Bc** White **Bl** Blue **J** Yellow **Mv** Mauve **Mr** Brown **N** Black **R** Red **Ve** Green **Vi** Violet

DYANE

133

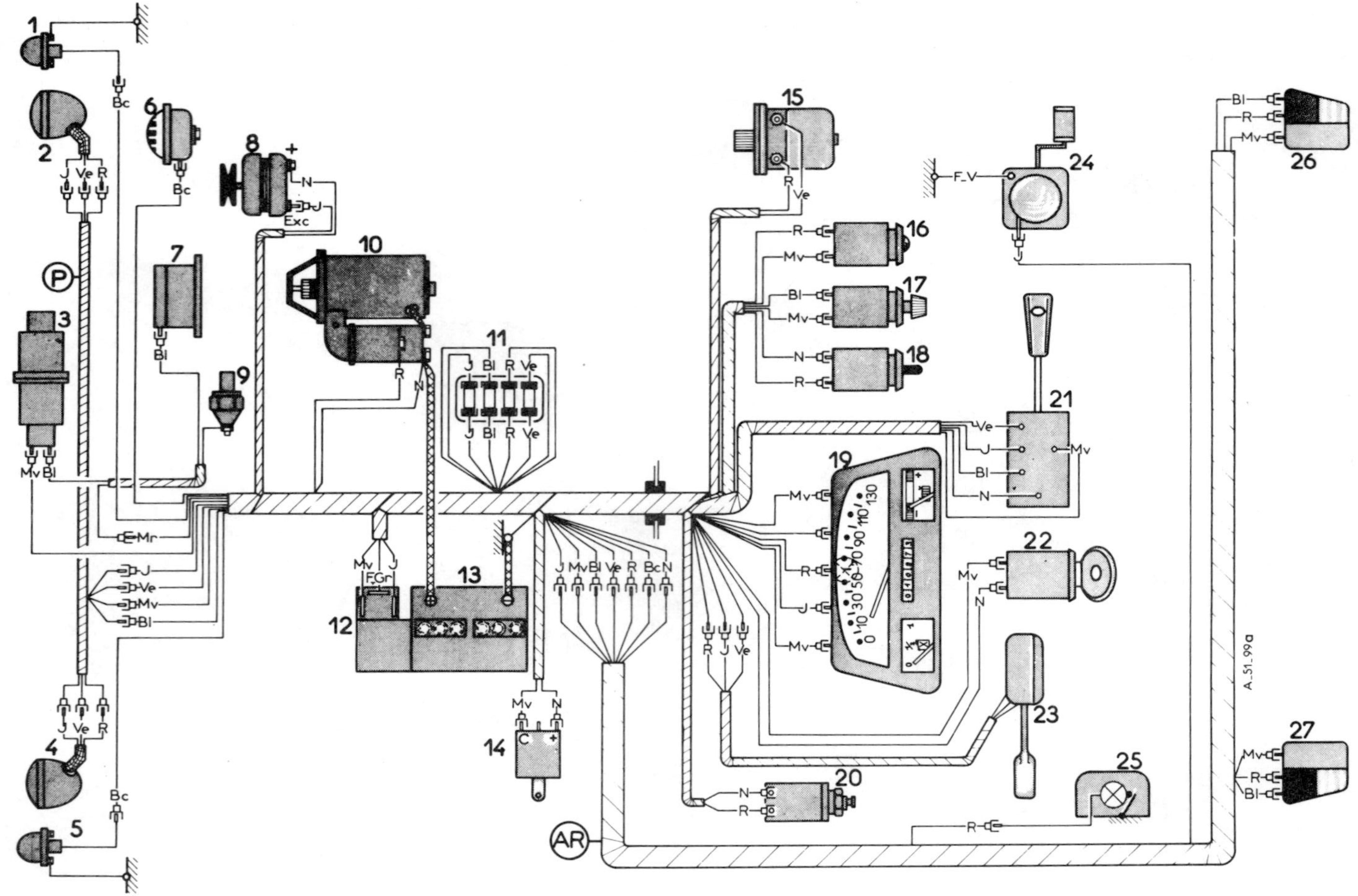

FIG 13:9 Wiring diagram 2CV4 and 6 (12-volt supply)

Key to Fig 13:9 1, 5 Direction indicators 2, 4 Headlamps 3 Coil 6 Horn 7 Distributor 8 Alternator 9 Oil pressure switch (2CV6) 10 Starter motor 11 Fuse box
12 Regulator 13 Battery 14 Flasher unit 15 Wiper motor 16 Oil pressure warning lamp (2CV6) 17 Wiper switch 18 Starter switch 19 Speedometer 20 Stop lamp
switch 21 Horn and lighting switch 22 Anti-theft ignition switch 23 Direction indicator switch 24 Fuel gauge rheostat 25 Interior lamp 26, 27 Rear lamp units

Colour code: **Bc** White **Bl** Blue **Gr** Grey **J** Yellow **Mr** Brown **Mv** Mauve **N** Black **R** Red **Ve** Green **F** Wire

134

HINTS ON MAINTENANCE AND OVERHAUL

There are few things more rewarding than the restoration of a vehicle's original peak of efficiency and smooth performance.

The following notes are intended to help the owner to reach that state of perfection. Providing that he possesses the basic manual skills he should have no difficulty in performing most of the operations detailed in this manual. It must be stressed, however, that where recommended in the manual, highly-skilled operations ought to be entrusted to experts, who have the necessary equipment, to carry out the work satisfactorily.

Quality of workmanship:

The hazardous driving conditions on the roads to-day demand that vehicles should be as nearly perfect, mechanically, as possible. It is therefore most important that amateur work be carried out with care, bearing in mind the often inadequate working conditions, and also the inferior tools which may have to be used. It is easy to counsel perfection in all things, and we recognize that it may be setting an impossibly high standard. We do, however, suggest that every care should be taken to ensure that a vehicle is as safe to take on the road as it is humanly possible to make it.

Safe working conditions:

Even though a vehicle may be stationary, it is still potentially dangerous if certain sensible precautions are not taken when working on it while it is supported on jacks or blocks. It is indeed preferable not to use jacks alone, but to supplement them with carefully placed blocks, so that there will be plenty of support if the car rolls off the jacks during a strenuous manoeuvre. Axle stands are an excellent way of providing a rigid base which is not readily disturbed. Piles of bricks are a dangerous substitute. Be careful not to get under heavy loads on lifting tackle, the load could fall. It is preferable not to work alone when lifting an engine, or when working underneath a vehicle which is supported well off the ground. To be trapped, particularly under the vehicle, may have unpleasant results if help is not quickly forthcoming. Make some provision, however humble, to deal with fires. Always disconnect a battery if there is a likelihood of electrical shorts. These may start a fire if there is leaking fuel about. This applies particularly to leads which can carry a heavy current, like those in the starter circuit. While on the subject of electricity, we must also stress the danger of using equipment which is run off the mains and which has no earth or has faulty wiring or connections. So many workshops have damp floors, and electrical shocks are of such a nature that it is sometimes impossible to let go of a live lead or piece of equipment due to the muscular spasms which take place.

Work demanding special care:

This involves the servicing of braking, steering and suspension systems. On the road, failure of the braking system may be disastrous. Make quite sure that there can be no possibility of failure through the bursting of rusty brake pipes or rotten hoses, nor to a sudden loss of pressure due to defective seals or valves.

Problems:

The chief problems which may face an operator are:
1 External dirt.
2 Difficulty in undoing tight fixings
3 Dismantling unfamiliar mechanisms.
4 Deciding in what respect parts are defective.
5 Confusion about the correct order for reassembly.
6 Adjusting running clearances.
7 Road testing.
8 Final tuning.

Practical suggestions to solve the problems:

1 Preliminary cleaning of large parts—engines, transmissions, steering, suspensions, etc.,—should be carried out before removal from the car. Where road dirt and mud alone are present, wash clean with a high-pressure water jet, brushing to remove stubborn adhesions, and allow to drain and dry. Where oil or grease is also present, wash down with a proprietary compound (Gunk, Teepol etc.,) applying with a stiff brush—an old paint brush is suitable—into all crevices. Cover the distributor and ignition coils with a polythene bag and then apply a strong water jet to clear the loosened deposits. Allow to drain and dry. The assemblies will then be sufficiently clean to remove and transfer to the bench for the next stage.

On the bench, further cleaning can be carried out, first wiping the parts as free as possible from grease with old newspaper. Avoid using rag or cotton waste which can leave clogging fibres behind. Any remaining grease can be removed with a brush dipped in paraffin. If necessary, traces of paraffin can be removed by carbon tetrachloride. Avoid using paraffin or petrol in large quantities for cleaning in enclosed areas, such as garages, on account of the high fire risk.

When all exteriors have been cleaned, and not before, dismantling can be commenced. This ensures that dirt will not enter into interiors and orifices revealed by dismantling. In the next phases, where components have to be cleaned, use carbon tetrachloride in preference to petrol and keep the containers covered except when in use. After the components have been cleaned, plug small holes with tapered hard wood plugs cut to size and blank off larger orifices with grease-proof paper and masking tape. Do not use soft wood plugs or matchsticks as they may break.

2 It is not advisable to hammer on the end of a screw thread, but if it must be done, first screw on a nut to protect the thread, and use a lead hammer. This applies particularly to the removal of tapered cotters. Nuts and bolts seem to 'grow' together, especially in exhaust systems. If penetrating oil does not work, try the judicious application of heat, but be careful of starting a fire. Asbestos sheet or cloth is useful to isolate heat.

Tight bushes or pieces of tail-pipe rusted into a silencer can be removed by splitting them with an open-ended hacksaw. Tight screws can sometimes be started by a tap from a hammer on the end of a suitable screwdriver. Many tight fittings will yield to the judicious use of a hammer, but it must be a soft-faced hammer if damage is to be avoided, use a heavy block on the opposite side to absorb shock. Any parts of the steering system which have been damaged should be renewed, as attempts to repair them may lead to cracking and subsequent failure, and steering ball joints should be disconnected using a recommended tool to prevent damage.

3 If often happens that an owner is baffled when trying to dismantle an unfamiliar piece of equipment. So many modern devices are pressed together or assembled by spinning-over flanges, that they must be sawn apart. The intention is that the whole assembly must be renewed. However, parts which appear to be in one piece to the naked eye, may reveal close-fitting joint lines when inspected with a magnifying glass, and, this may provide the necessary clue to dismantling. Left-handed screw threads are used where rotational forces would tend to unscrew a right-handed screw thread.

Be very careful when dismantling mechanisms which may come apart suddenly. Work in an enclosed space where the parts will be contained, and drape a piece of cloth over the device if springs are likely to fly in all directions. Mark everything which might be reassembled in the wrong position, scratched symbols may be used on unstressed parts, or a sequence of tiny dots from a centre punch can be useful. Stressed parts should never be scratched or centre-popped as this may lead to cracking under working conditions. Store parts which look alike in the correct order for reassembly. Never rely upon memory to assist in the assembly of complicated mechanisms, especially when they will be dismantled for a long time, but make notes, and drawings to supplement the diagrams in the manual, and put labels on detached wires. Rust stains may indicate unlubricated wear. This can sometimes be seen round the outside edge of a bearing cup in a universal joint. Look for bright rubbing marks on parts which normally should not make heavy contact. These might prove that something is bent or running out of truth. For example, there might be bright marks on one side of a piston, at the top near the ring grooves, and others at the bottom of the skirt on the other side. This could well be the clue to a bent connecting rod. Suspected cracks can be proved by heating the component in a light oil to approximately 100°C, removing, drying off, and dusting with french chalk, if a crack is present the oil retained in the crack will stain the french chalk.

4 In determining wear, and the degree, against the permissible limits set in the manual, accurate measurement can only be achieved by the use of a micrometer. In many cases, the wear is given to the fourth place of decimals; that is in ten-thousandths of an inch. This can be read by the vernier scale on the barrel of a good micrometer. Bore diameters are more difficult to determine. If, however, the matching shaft is accurately measured, the degree of play in the bore can be felt as a guide to its suitability. In other cases, the shank of a twist drill of known diameter is a handy check.

Many methods have been devised for determining the clearance between bearing surfaces. To-day the best and simplest is by the use of Plastigage, obtainable from most garages. A thin plastic thread is laid between the two surfaces and the bearing is tightened, flattening the thread. On removal, the width of the thread is compared with a scale supplied with the thread and the clearance is read off directly. Sometimes joint faces leak persistently, even after gasket renewal. The fault will then be traceable to distortion, dirt or burrs. Studs which are screwed into soft metal frequently raise burrs at the point of entry. A quick cure for this is to chamfer the edge of the hole in the part which fits over the stud.

5 **Always check a replacement part with the original one before it is fitted.**

If parts are not marked, and the order for reassembly is not known, a little detective work will help. Look for marks which are due to wear to see if they can be mated. Joint faces may not be identical due to manufacturing errors, and parts which overlap may be stained, giving a clue to the correct position. Most fixings leave identifying marks especially if they were painted over on assembly. It is then easier to decide whether a nut, for instance, has a plain, a spring, or a shakeproof washer under it. All running surfaces become 'bedded' together after long spells of work and tiny imperfections on one part will be found to have left corresponding marks on the other. This is particularly true of shafts and bearings and even a score on a cylinder wall will show on the piston.

6 Checking end float or rocker clearances by feeler gauge may not always give accurate results because of wear. For instance, the rocker tip which bears on a valve stem may be deeply pitted, in which case the feeler will simply be bridging a depression. Thrust washers may also wear depressions in opposing faces to make accurate measurement difficult. End float is then easier to check by using a dial gauge. It is common practice to adjust end play in bearing assemblies, like front hubs with taper rollers, by doing up the axle nut until the hub becomes stiff to turn and then backing it off a little. Do not use this method with ballbearing hubs as the assembly is often preloaded by tightening the axle nut to its fullest extent. If the splitpin hole will not line up, file the base of the nut a little.

Steering assemblies often wear in the straight-ahead position. If any part is adjusted, make sure that it remains free when moved from lock to lock. Do not be surprised if an assembly like a steering gearbox, which is known to be carefully adjusted outside the car, becomes stiff when it is bolted in place. This will be due to distortion of the case by the pull of the mounting bolts, particularly if the mounting points are not all touching together. This problem may be met in other equipment and is cured by careful attention to the alignment of mounting points.

When a spanner is stamped with a size and A/F it means that the dimension is the width between the jaws and has no connection with ANF, which is the designation for the American National Fine thread. Coarse threads like Whitworth are rarely used on cars to-day except for studs which screw into soft aluminium or cast iron. For this reason it might be found that the top end of a cylinder head stud has a fine thread and the lower end a coarse thread to screw into the cylinder block. If the car has mainly UNF threads then it is likely that any coarse threads will be UNC, which are not the same as Whitworth. Small sizes have the same number of threads in Whitworth and UNC, but in the $\frac{1}{2}$ inch size for example, there are twelve threads to the inch in the former and thirteen in the latter.

7 After a major overhaul, particularly if a great deal of work has been done on the braking, steering and suspension systems, it is advisable to approach the problem of testing with care. If the braking system has been overhauled, apply heavy pressure to the brake pedal and get a second operator to check every possible source of leakage. The brakes may work extremely well, but a leak could cause complete failure after a few miles.

Do not fit the hub caps until every wheel nut has been checked for tightness, and make sure the tyre pressures are correct. Check the levels of coolant, lubricants and hydraulic fluids. Being satisfied that all is well, take the car on the road and test the brakes at once. Check the steering and the action of the handbrake. Do all this at moderate speeds on quiet roads, and make sure there is no other vehicle behind you when you try a rapid stop.

Finally, remember that many parts settle down after a time, so check for tightness of all fixings after the car has been on the road for a hundred miles or so.

8 It is useless to tune an engine which has not reached its normal running temperature. In the same way, the tune of an engine which is stiff after a rebore will be different when the engine is again running free. Remember too, that rocker clearances on pushrod operated valve gear will change when the cylinder head nuts are tightened after an initial period of running with a new head gasket.

Trouble may not always be due to what seems the obvious cause. Ignition, carburation and mechanical condition are interdependent and spitting back through the carburetter, which might be attributed to a weak mixture, can be caused by a sticking inlet valve.

For one final hint on tuning, never adjust more than one thing at a time or it will be impossible to tell which adjustment produced the desired result.

NOTES

GLOSSARY OF TERMS

Allen key — Cranked wrench of hexagonal section for use with socket head screws.

Alternator — Electrical generator producing alternating current. Rectified to direct current for battery charging.

Ambient temperature — Surrounding atmospheric temperature.

Annulus — Used in engineering to indicate the outer ring gear of an epicyclic gear train.

Armature — The shaft carrying the windings, which rotates in the magnetic field of a generator or starter motor. That part of a solenoid or relay which is activated by the magnetic field.

Axial — In line with, or pertaining to, an axis.

Backlash — Play in meshing gears.

Balance lever — A bar where force applied at the centre is equally divided between connections at the ends.

Banjo axle — Axle casing with large diameter housing for the crownwheel and differential.

Bendix pinion — A self-engaging and self-disengaging drive on a starter motor shaft.

Bevel pinion — A conical shaped gearwheel, designed to mesh with a similar gear with an axis usually at 90 deg. to its own.

bhp — Brake horse power, measured on a dynamometer.

bmep — Brake mean effective pressure. Average pressure on a piston during the working stroke.

Brake cylinder — Cylinder with hydraulically operated piston(s) acting on brake shoes or pad(s).

Brake regulator — Control valve fitted in hydraulic braking system which limits brake pressure to rear brakes during heavy braking to prevent rear wheel locking.

Camber — Angle at which a wheel is tilted from the vertical.

Capacitor — Modern term for an electrical condenser. Part of distributor assembly, connected across contact breaker points, acts as an interference suppressor.

Castellated — Top face of a nut, slotted across the flats, to take a locking splitpin.

Castor — Angle at which the kingpin or swivel pin is tilted when viewed from the side.

cc — Cubic centimetres. Engine capacity is arrived at by multiplying the area of the bore in sq cm by the stroke in cm by the number of cylinders.

Clevis — U-shaped forked connector used with a clevis pin, usually at handbrake connections.

Celsius — Degree Celsius (°C) is the metric practical unit of temperature formerly called Centigrade.

Collet — A type of collar, usually split and located in a groove in a shaft, and held in place by a retainer. The arrangement used to retain the spring(s) on a valve stem in most cases.

Commutator — Rotating segmented current distributor between armature windings and brushes in generator or motor.

Compression ratio — The ratio, or quantitative relation, of the total volume (piston at bottom of stroke) to the unswept volume (piston at top of stroke) in an engine cylinder.

Condenser — See capacitor.

Core plug — Plug for blanking off a manufacturing hole in a casting.

Cr — Compression ratio

Crownwheel — Large bevel gear in rear axle, driven by a bevel pinion attached to the propeller shaft. Sometimes called a 'ring gear'.

'C'-spanner — Like a 'C' with a handle. For use on screwed collars without flats, but with slots or holes.

Damper — Modern term for shock-absorber, used in vehicle suspension systems to damp out spring oscillations.

Depression — The lowering of atmospheric pressure as in the inlet manifold and carburetter.

Dowel — Close tolerance pin, peg, tube, or bolt, which accurately locates mating parts.

Drag link — Rod connecting steering box drop arm (pitman arm) to nearest front wheel steering arm in certain types of steering systems.

Dry liner — Thinwall tube pressed into cylinder bore

Dry sump — Lubrication system where all oil is scavenged from the sump, and returned to a separate tank.

Dynamo — See Generator.

Electrode — Terminal, part of an electrical component, such as the points or 'Electrodes' of a sparking plug.

Electrolyte — In lead-acid car batteries a solution of sulphuric acid and distilled water.

End float — The axial movement between associated parts, end play.

EP — Extreme pressure. In lubricants, special grades for heavily loaded bearing surfaces, such as gear teeth in a gearbox, or crownwheel and pinion in a rear axle.

Fade	Of brakes. Reduced efficiency due to overheating.
Field coils	Windings on the polepieces of motors and generators.
Fillets	Narrow finishing strips usually applied to interior bodywork.
First motion shaft	Input shaft from clutch to gearbox.
Fullflow filter	Filters in which all the oil is pumped to the engine. If the element becomes clogged, a bypass valve operates to pass unfiltered oil to the engine.
FWD	Front wheel drive.
g	Gramme.
Gear pump	Two meshing gears in a close fitting casing. Oil is carried from the inlet round the outside of both gears in the spaces between the gear teeth and casing to the outlet, the meshing gear teeth prevent oil passing back to the inlet, and the oil is forced through the outlet port.
Generator	Modern term for 'Dynamo'. When rotated produces electrical current.
Grommet	A ring of protective or sealing material. Can be used to protect pipes or leads passing through bulkheads.
Grubscrew	Fully threaded headless screw with screwdriver slot. Used for locking, or alignment purposes.
Gudgeon pin	Shaft which connects a piston to its connecting rod. Sometimes called 'wrist pin', or 'piston pin'.
Halfshaft	One of a pair transmitting drive from the differential.
Helical	In spiral form. The teeth of helical gears are cut at a spiral angle to the side faces of the gearwheel.
Hot spot	Hot area that assists vapourisation of fuel on its way to cylinders. Often provided by close contact between inlet and exhaust manifolds.
HT	High Tension. Applied to electrical current produced by the ignition coil for the sparking plugs.
Hydrometer	A device for checking specific gravity of liquids. Used to check specific gravity of electrolyte.
Hypoid bevel gears	A form of bevel gear used in the rear axle drive gears. The bevel pinion meshes below the centre line of the crownwheel, giving a lower propeller shaft line.
Idler	A device for passing on movement. A free running gear between driving and driven gears. A lever transmitting track rod movement to a side rod in steering gear.
Impeller	A centrifugal pumping element. Used in water pumps to stimulate flow.
Journals	Those parts of a shaft that are in contact with the bearings.
kg	Kilogramme.
kg m	Metric measure of twist or torque. A pull of 10 kg at a radius of 1 m is a torque of 10 kg m.
kg/sq/cm	Kilogrammes per square centimetre.
Kingpin	The main vertical pin which carries the front wheel spindle, and permits steering movement. May be called 'steering pin' or 'swivel pin'.
Layshaft	The shaft which carries the laygear in the gearbox. The laygear is driven by the first motion shaft and drives the third motion shaft according to the gear selected. Sometimes called the 'countershaft' or 'second motion shaft.'
lb ft	A measure of twist or torque. A pull of 10 lb at a radius of 1 ft is a torque of 10 lb ft.
lb/sq in	Pounds per square inch.
Little-end	The small, or piston end of a connecting rod. Sometimes called the 'small-end'.
LT	Low Tension. The current output from the battery.
m	Metre.
Mandrel	Accurately manufactured bar or rod used for test or centring purposes.
Manifold	A pipe, duct, or chamber, with several branches.
Needle rollers	Bearing rollers with a length many times their diameter.
Oil bath	Reservoir which lubricates parts by immersion. In air filters, a separate oil supply for wetting a wire mesh element to hold the dust.
Oil wetted	In air filters, a wire mesh element lightly oiled to trap and hold airborne dust.
Overlap	Period during which inlet and exhaust valves are open together.
Panhard rod	Bar connected between fixed point on chassis and another on axle to control sideways movement.
Pawl	Pivoted catch which engages in the teeth of a ratchet to permit movement in one direction only.
Peg spanner	Tool with pegs, or pins, to engage in holes or slots in the part to be turned.
Pendant pedals	Pedals with levers that are pivoted at the top end.
Phillips screwdriver	A cross-point screwdriver for use with the cross-slotted heads of Phillips screws.

Pinion	A small gear, usually in relation to another gear.	**Stub axle**	Short axle fixed at one end only.
Piston-type damper	Shock absorber in which damping is controlled by a piston working in a closed oil-filled cylinder.	**Tachometer**	An instrument for accurate measurement of rotating speed. Usually indicates in revolutions per minute.
Preloading	Preset static pressure on ball or roller bearings not due to working loads.	**TDC**	Top Dead Centre. The highest point reached by a piston in a cylinder, with the crank and connecting rod in line.
Radial	Radiating from a centre, like the spokes of a wheel.	**Thermostat**	Automatic device for regulating temperature. Used in vehicle coolant systems to open a valve which restricts circulation at low temperature.
Radius rod	Pivoted arm confining movement of a part to an arc of fixed radius.	**Third motion shaft**	Output shaft of gearbox.
Ratchet	Toothed wheel or rack which can move in one direction only, movement in the other being prevented by a pawl.	**Threequarter floating axle**	Outer end of rear axle halfshaft flanged and bolted to wheel hub, which runs on bearing mounted on outside of axle casing. Vehicle weight is not carried by the axle shaft.
Ring gear	A gear tooth ring attached to outer periphery of flywheel. Starter pinion engages with it during starting.		
Runout	Amount by which rotating part is out of true.	**Thrust bearing or washer**	Used to reduce friction in rotating parts subject to axial loads.
Semi-floating axle	Outer end of rear axle halfshaft is carried on bearing inside axle casing. Wheel hub is secured to end of shaft.	**Torque**	Turning or twisting effort. See 'lb ft'.
		Track rod	The bar(s) across the vehicle which connect the steering arms and maintain the front wheels in their correct alignment.
Servo	A hydraulic or pneumatic system for assisting, or, augmenting a physical effort. See 'Vacuum Servo'.		
		UJ	Universal joint. A coupling between shafts which permits angular movement.
Setscrew	One which is threaded for the full length of the shank.		
Shackle	A coupling link, used in the form of two parallel pins connected by side plates to secure the end of the master suspension spring and absorb the effects of deflection.	**UNF**	Unified National Fine screw thread.
		Vacuum servo	Device used in brake system, using difference between atmospheric pressure and inlet manifold depression to operate a piston which acts to augment brake pressure as required. See 'Servo'.
Shell bearing	Thinwalled steel shell lined with anti-friction metal. Usually semi-circular and used in pairs for main and big-end bearings.		
		Venturi	A restriction or 'choke' in a tube, as in a carburetter, used to increase velocity to obtain a reduction in pressure.
Shock absorber	See 'Damper'.		
Silentbloc	Rubber bush bonded to inner and outer metal sleeves.	**Vernier**	A sliding scale for obtaining fractional readings of the graduations of an adjacent scale.
Socket-head screw	Screw with hexagonal socket for an Allen key.	**Welch plug**	A domed thin metal disc which is partially flattened to lock in a recess. Used to plug core holes in castings.
Solenoid	A coil of wire creating a magnetic field when electric current passes through it. Used with a soft iron core to operate contacts or a mechanical device.	**Wet liner**	Removable cylinder barrel, sealed against coolant leakage, where the coolant is in direct contact with the outer surface.
Spur gear	A gear with teeth cut axially across the periphery.	**Wet sump**	A reservoir attached to the crankcase to hold the lubricating oil.

NOTES

INDEX